A BOOK OF
DISCOVERY &
LEARNING

The Incredible Human Body

Fran Balkwill & Mic Rolph

Sterling Publishing Co., Inc.
New York

Library of Congress Cataloging-in-Publication Data
Balkwill, Frances R.
    The incredible human body : a book of discovery & learning / Fran Balkwill &
Mic Rolph
        p.   cm.
    Originally published as: The great egg and sperm race. Great Britain :
Collins, © 1996.
    Includes index.
    ISBN 0-8069-6125-2
    1. Human biology.   Popular works.   I. Rolph, Mic.   II. Title.
QP38.B197   1996
612–dc20   96-25745
                                                                                        CIP

1   3   5   7   9   10   8   6   4   2

Published 1996 by Sterling Publishing Company, Inc.
387 Park Avenue South, New York, N.Y. 10016
Originally published in Great Britain by HarperCollins Children's Books
a division of HarperCollins Publishers, under the title *The Great Egg and Sperm
Race*
Text © 1994 by Fran Balkwill
Illustrations © 1994 by Mic Rolph
Distributed in Canada by Sterling Publishing
% Canadian Manda Group, One Atlantic Avenue, Suite 105
Toronto, Ontario, Canada M6K 3E7

Sterling ISBN 0-8069-6125-2

Printed in Hong Kong

Contents

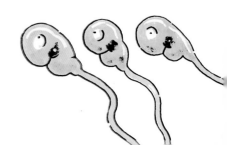

Way Back When

You are an incredibly sophisticated and complicated machine, a machine that took billions of years to develop. Its raw materials came from the dust of the stars. This is the story of that machine, the story of the human body.

Our story begins beyond the limits of human imagination. There was nothing. No time, no space, no energy, no matter, no gravity.

But just then, about fifteen billion
years ago…

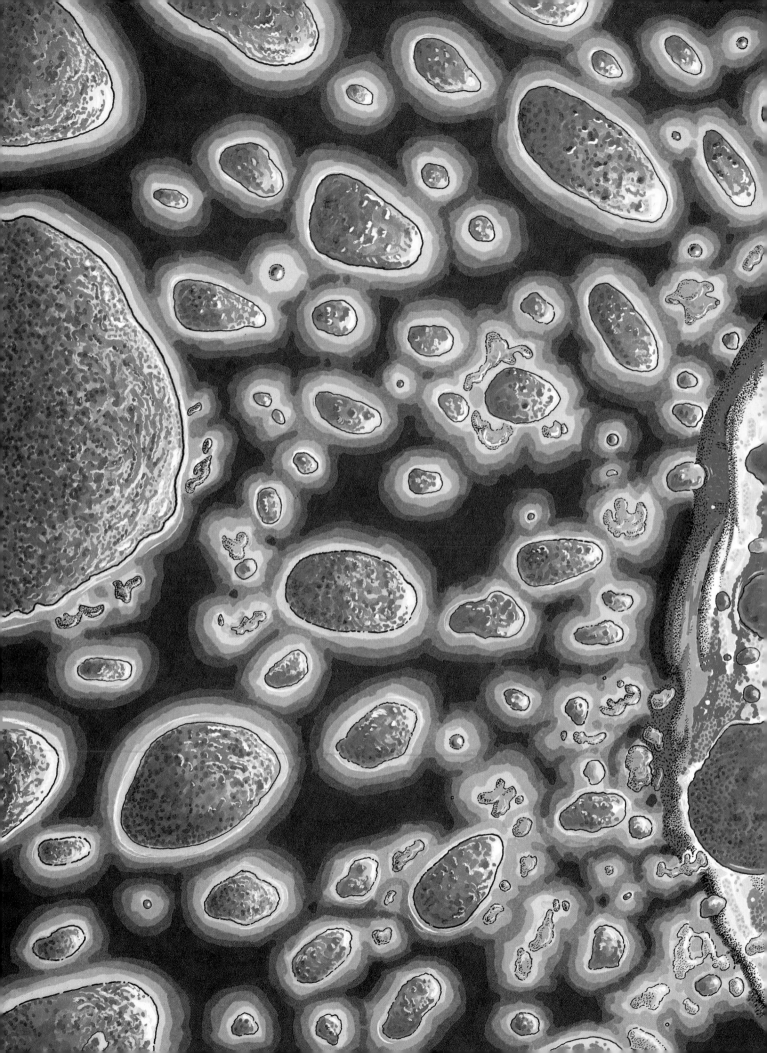

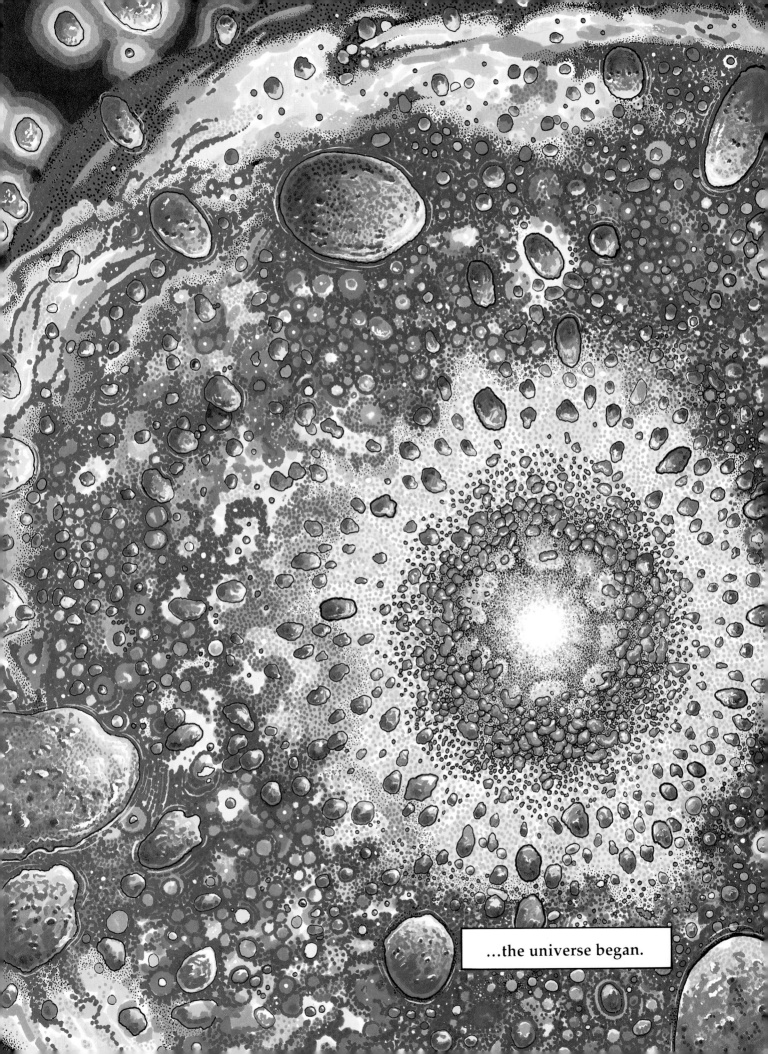

...the universe began.

Less than one billionth of a second later, the universe started to expand and cool. Spinning clouds of luminous gas reeled ever outwards and onwards from the center leaving vast empty spaces between them. In some places the gas clouds were thicker and stopped expanding. They slowly shrank to become the birthplaces of stars that lit the vast darkness. The universe became a mass of galaxies, each made of millions of fiery stars. About four and a half billion years ago, in a spiral galaxy of some hundred thousand million stars, a new star was born, a star we now call our Sun.

All around the new star was a rim of gases and dust. Some of this stardust and gas fused into enormous boulders. The boulders collided – often quite violently so that they shattered on impact – but sometimes more gently so they joined together. By the time the Sun was one hundred million years old, the boulders had formed comets, planets and satellites.

The third planet from the Sun had a thick layer of gases above its surface, and a very large satellite orbiting around it. That planet is your home, the Earth, its satellite, the Moon.

9

The early Earth was a strange and violent place. Thunder and lightning filled its swirling skies. The surface was continually rocked by earthquakes and erupting volcanoes. Planet Earth slowly began to cool and solidify. It was not too hot, like those planets closer to the Sun, nor too cold, like those further away. The Sun's heat that warmed the Earth was trapped by its atmosphere. This atmosphere also protected the surface of the Earth from many of the harmful rays that came from the Sun.

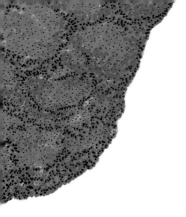

Steam condensed and began to fall from the skies as rain, cleansing much of the volcanic dust from the atmosphere and forming raging torrents, which emptied into vast oceans and seas.

Planet Earth now had water which allowed a number of extraordinary chemical reactions to take place in the seas over many millions of years. Gases and simple chemicals formed many strange and complex substances under the influence of lightning and sun rays. Some of these chemicals may even have come from asteroids, meteorites or comets that often collided with the young Earth.

The chemical substances became enclosed in thin membranes, a bit like soap bubbles. Inside the membranes the chemicals behaved differently from those in the world outside. These were the first cells on our planet. The cells could grow and increase in number by making copies of themselves. They could even react to changes in the extremely harsh world outside. Life had begun, in the form of minute creatures each made of just one cell.

We now call these cells bacteria (*bac-tear-ia*) and algae (*al-gee*). Floating on the surface of the seas, some of the microscopic creatures were able to trap energy from sunlight and make the gas oxygen (*ox-ee-jen*). The slow buildup of oxygen allowed many other life forms to develop. Over millions of years, the single cells of bacteria and algae joined together to make plants and animals, first made of hundreds, then thousands, then millions of cells.

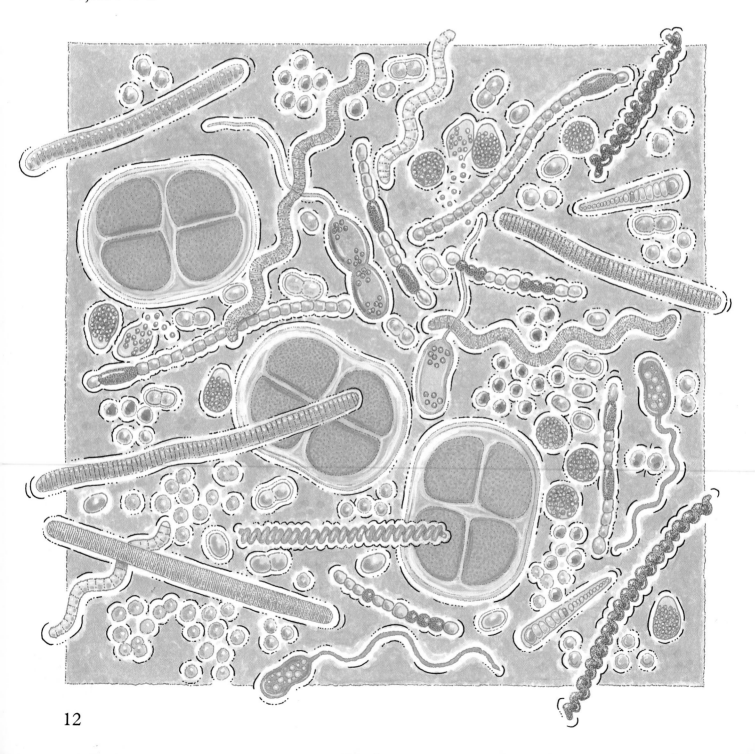

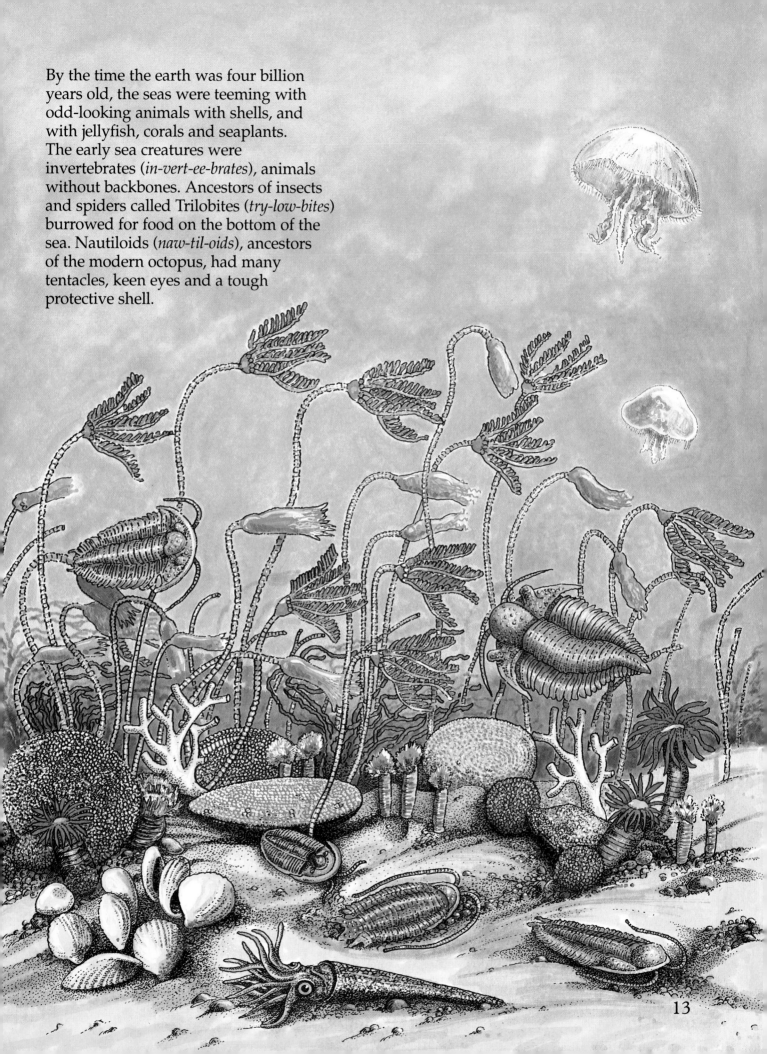

By the time the earth was four billion years old, the seas were teeming with odd-looking animals with shells, and with jellyfish, corals and seaplants. The early sea creatures were invertebrates (*in-vert-ee-brates*), animals without backbones. Ancestors of insects and spiders called Trilobites (*try-low-bites*) burrowed for food on the bottom of the sea. Nautiloids (*naw-til-oids*), ancestors of the modern octopus, had many tentacles, keen eyes and a tough protective shell.

The first vertebrates (animals with backbones) were fish. They had no fins and sucked or sieved their food. Jaws evolved so that fish, some as long as thirty feet, could crunch and bite their prey. Some four hundred million years ago, sea plants began to grow and cling onto the lifeless rocky landscape. These plants gave off more and more oxygen, allowing animals to crawl out of the seas and live and breathe on land as well. Millipedes, worms, and primitive insects appeared to feed on the land plants.

When these plants and animals died and rotted, the first patches of soil formed on the barren rock. Fish fins became feet, animals began to gulp in air, and the first vertebrates took to the land. These were amphibians, ancestors of frogs and salamanders, but they still returned to the seas to lay their eggs.

It took another fifty million years or so for winged insects to fly. Then came the age of the reptiles, who laid their eggs on dry land.

The undoubted kings were dinosaurs and they dominated the planet for over one hundred and fifty million years. They came in an amazing number of shapes and sizes, some as small as chickens, others much larger than any land animal alive today. The first birds flew and the first mammals, small shrew-like creatures, lived among flowering plants and trees. Their young developed inside their bodies, and after they were born they fed on their mothers' milk. But dinosaurs still ruled the land, until, within the space of a million years or so, they vanished, along with many other creatures of that time. Some scientists think that a gigantic meteorite struck the planet, or volcanic eruptions changed the climate. Others think that dinosaurs were smitten with a terrible disease, that a plague of caterpillars ate their food, or that some newly-evolved mammals ate all their eggs!

The disappearance of the dinosaurs was not a unique event in the history of our planet. In fact, there have been at least six mass extinctions of life in the last five hundred million years. These may have been caused by ice ages, global warming or by a storm of giant comets and meteorites. Huge changes in the environment may destroy over ninety percent of species, but some creatures are able to survive in the new surroundings and form the next stage of evolution. Crocodiles, birds and mammals survived the destruction of the dinosaurs, but many new species appeared. Mammals, especially large mammals, soon became the most successful.

About twenty million years ago ape-like mammals lived in trees in tropical forests and woodland. About sixteen million years later some began to walk upright on two legs. The shape of the bones in their hips, knees and feet changed and their arms became shorter than their legs. This allowed them to travel greater distances and move faster. Their hands, freed from helping them move along the ground, developed a powerful, precise grip. Two and a half million years ago the climate cooled and woodlands and forests were replaced by vast open stretches of grasslands. The apes that survived this change had also developed much larger brains.

They looked a bit like modern humans, but their forehead was low and sloping, their eyebrows rested on bulging bony ridges, shielding their eyes in deep sockets. Their nose, jaw and massive teeth protruded far forward – but they had no chin. Their muscles would have been the envy of a bodybuilder and their handshake would have been bone crunching!

They discovered the secret of making fire and must have fashioned simple clothing as the world was in the grip of an ice age. They also made simple tools of stone and wood. For a million years or so these primitive humans lived by hunting animals in packs.

What happened next is not so certain, but (probably) about one hundred thousand years ago in Africa, some of these early humans began to evolve and look much more like we do today.

They were the first members of our species, *Homo sapiens* (*sap-ee-ens*), and had high foreheads and well-developed chins. About fifty thousand years ago, humans began to spread into Europe and Asia. The primitive humans already living there didn't stand a chance. The invading tribes had greater intelligence and many new tools. And, maybe the most important difference of all, changes in their tongues and throat meant that they began to communicate with each other by talking in complex languages.

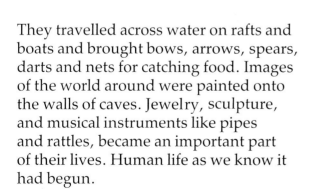

They travelled across water on rafts and boats and brought bows, arrows, spears, darts and nets for catching food. Images of the world around were painted onto the walls of caves. Jewelry, sculpture, and musical instruments like pipes and rattles, became an important part of their lives. Human life as we know it had begun.

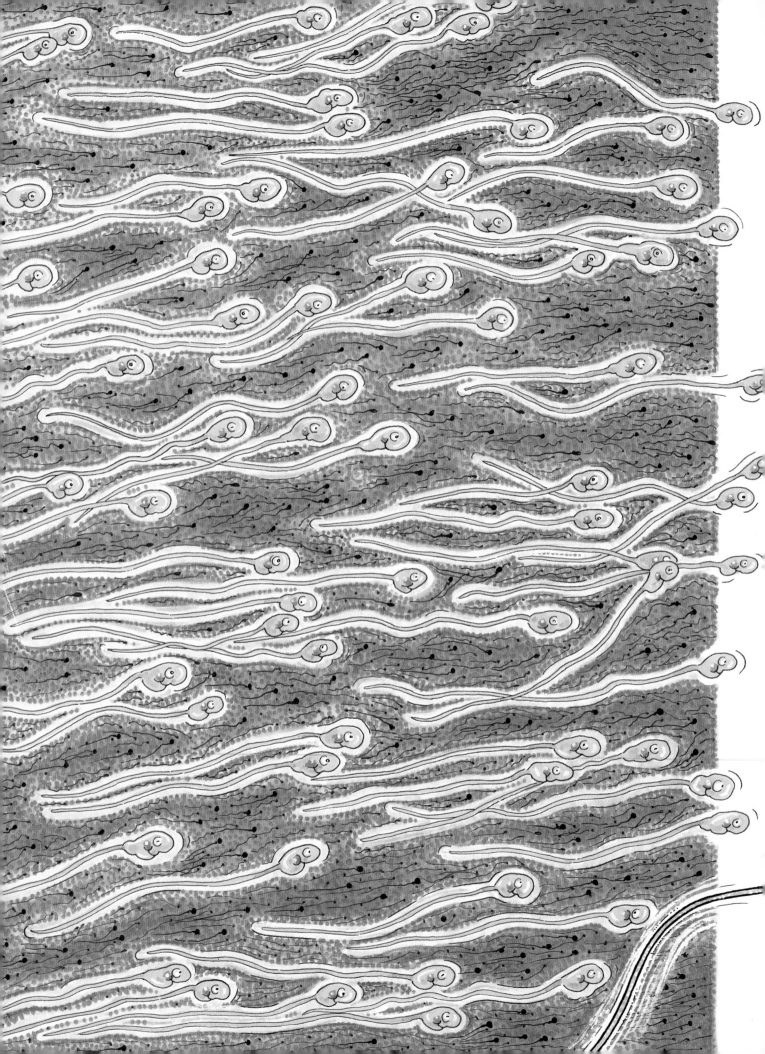

One and One Makes You

And then, about two thousand generations later, something very important happened. Two cells collided – one big, one small. The big cell, the egg, and the small cell, the sperm, became one very special cell…**YOU!**

When you set out on your life you looked like most other animals that live on our planet. You were just one single tiny cell, smaller than a grain of sand. But that cell had all the necessary instructions to make you as you are today. The cell was just large enough to be seen with the naked eye. If you peer very closely at the end of this sentence, you might be able to see a very tiny period about four thousandths of an inch wide

That is the size you were when you were first made!

Cells are the building blocks of your body. You are now made of millions. How can you see what they really look like? Your eyes are not powerful enough! From the earliest times, humans have been trying to find out more about the world inside and around them by using magnifying machines. Trying to see the cells of your body is like trying to see the stars in the sky. There are about one hundred thousand million stars in our galaxy alone. For four hundred years humans have searched the skies with telescopes to learn about outer space. They have also learned about inner space with another magnifying machine, the microscope.

This type of telescope was used by Galileo Galilei. The picture of the moon is a copy of his original drawing. You can't see much detail, but remember this was drawn in 1610.

The first microscopes revealed very little detail about cells, but nowadays most microscopes can make cells one thousand times bigger than they really are. Very special powerful electron microscopes can show us what goes on deep inside a cell by magnifying it more than ten thousand times!

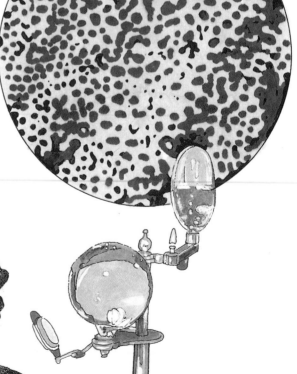

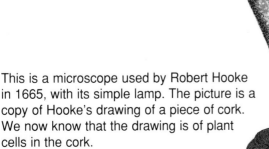

This is a microscope used by Robert Hooke in 1665, with its simple lamp. The picture is a copy of Hooke's drawing of a piece of cork. We now know that the drawing is of plant cells in the cork.

The first cell that was you was rather
large. Most cells in your body are only
four ten thousandths of an inch wide.
Look at your fingers. They are each about
ten thousand cells wide. How many cells
do you think it takes to make a finger?
Ten thousand? One million? Ten million?
No! Each of your fingers is made of
about ten thousand million cells! So you
can realize how small cells are! If each of
your cells was three eighths of an inch
wide, your little finger would be taller
than a two-story house!

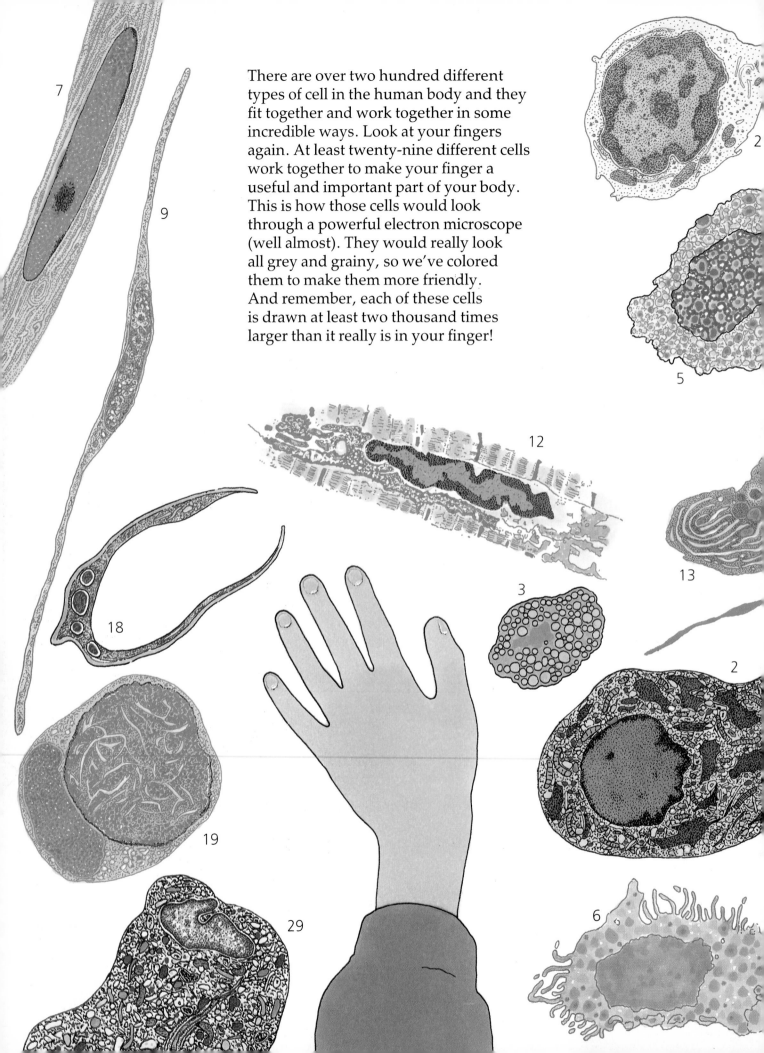

There are over two hundred different types of cell in the human body and they fit together and work together in some incredible ways. Look at your fingers again. At least twenty-nine different cells work together to make your finger a useful and important part of your body. This is how those cells would look through a powerful electron microscope (well almost). They would really look all grey and grainy, so we've colored them to make them more friendly. And remember, each of these cells is drawn at least two thousand times larger than it really is in your finger!

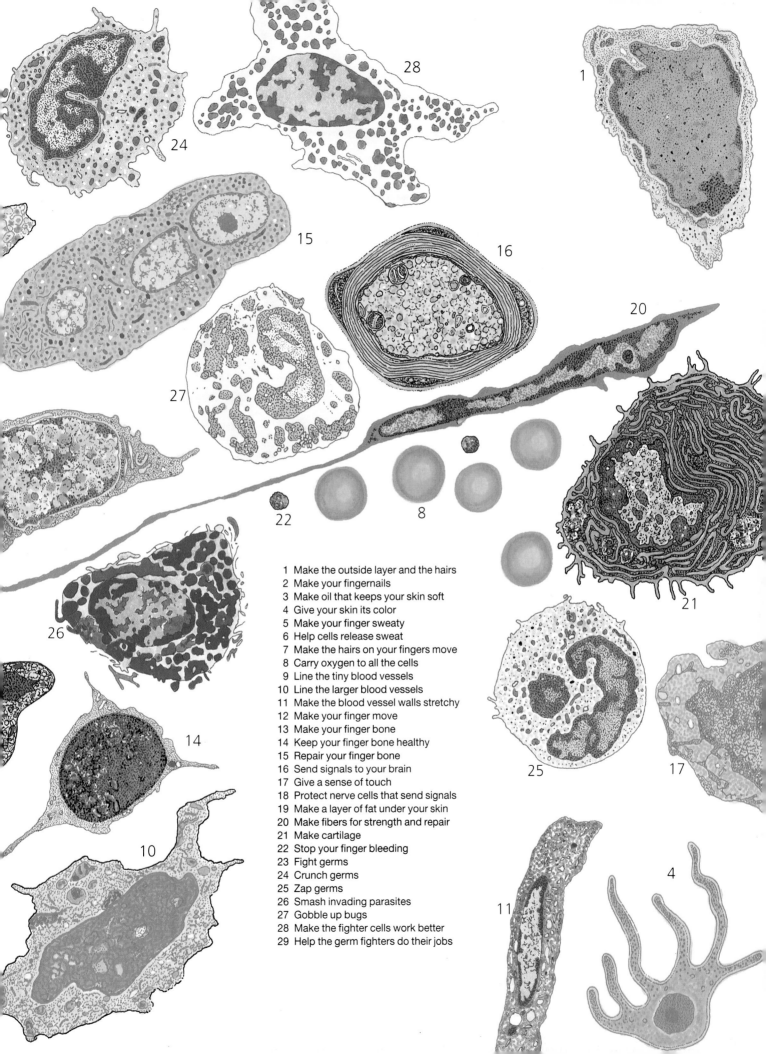

1 Make the outside layer and the hairs
2 Make your fingernails
3 Make oil that keeps your skin soft
4 Give your skin its color
5 Make your finger sweaty
6 Help cells release sweat
7 Make the hairs on your fingers move
8 Carry oxygen to all the cells
9 Line the tiny blood vessels
10 Line the larger blood vessels
11 Make the blood vessel walls stretchy
12 Make your finger move
13 Make your finger bone
14 Keep your finger bone healthy
15 Repair your finger bone
16 Send signals to your brain
17 Give a sense of touch
18 Protect nerve cells that send signals
19 Make a layer of fat under your skin
20 Make fibers for strength and repair
21 Make cartilage
22 Stop your finger bleeding
23 Fight germs
24 Crunch germs
25 Zap germs
26 Smash invading parasites
27 Gobble up bugs
28 Make the fighter cells work better
29 Help the germ fighters do their jobs

The total number of cells in your body is about one hundred million million. How did you get that many from just one tiny cell? Well, the first cell that was you grew a bit and then it divided and became two cells. Those two cells became four cells, those four cells became eight cells, and so on until you were made of billions. But first, let's see how cells work.

Although cells do many different jobs in your body, most of them have the same things inside them. This is what one of your liver cells looks like through an electron microscope. It is drawn about ten thousand times larger than it really is.

The chemicals that make all cells are, of course, the chemicals that make you. These are the chemicals that were made in the molten seas of the early planet billions of years ago, the chemicals of life. Inside each cell you find:

Proteins (*pro-teens*) that make cells the size and shape they are. Proteins help the cell do many of the jobs it has to do.

Carbohydrates (*car-bow-high-drates*). They are fuel that makes energy for the cell to work. As a car burns gas and oxygen to make it go, your cells use carbohydrates and oxygen

Fats that can generate energy but also make the important membranes inside and surrounding cells.

Salt and other simple chemicals in tiny amounts.

Vitamins which are vital for life because they help proteins do their jobs efficiently.

Complicated chemicals called **nucleic acids** (*new-clee-ick acids*) that contain instructions that control the cell.

Lots and lots of **water**.

As well as the chemicals, you can see that there are many strange shaped objects, squiggly tubes, and black dots and splotches inside this cell. What are they all and what jobs do they do?

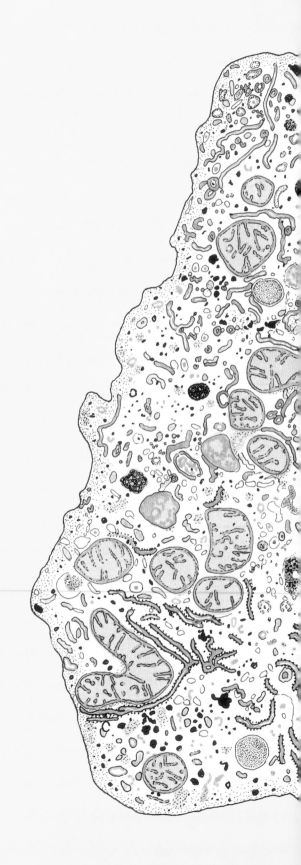

24

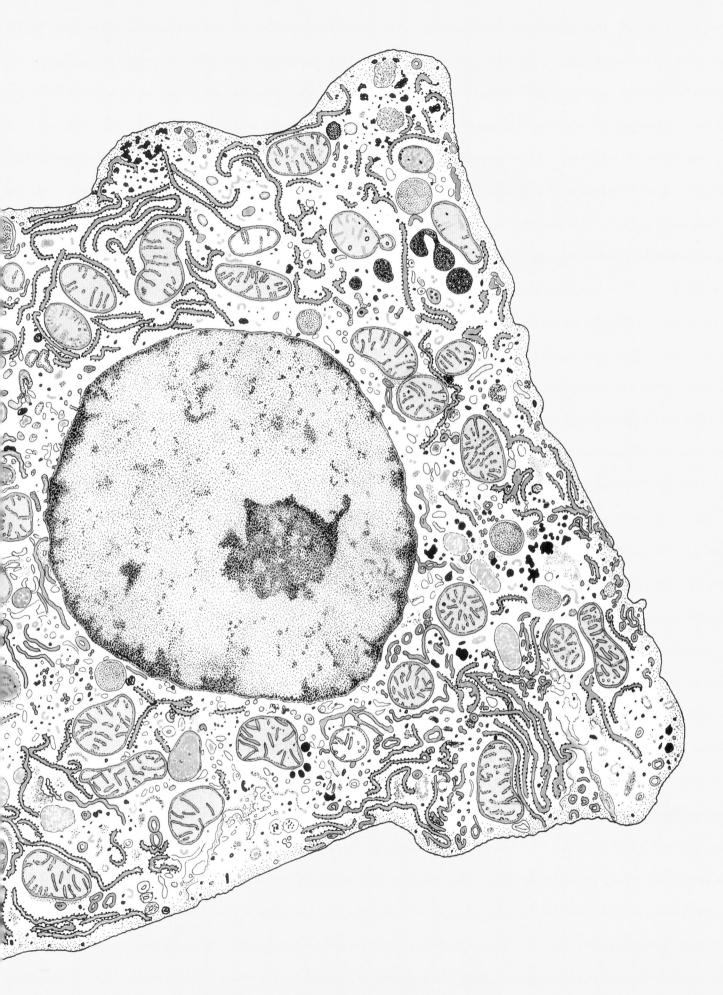

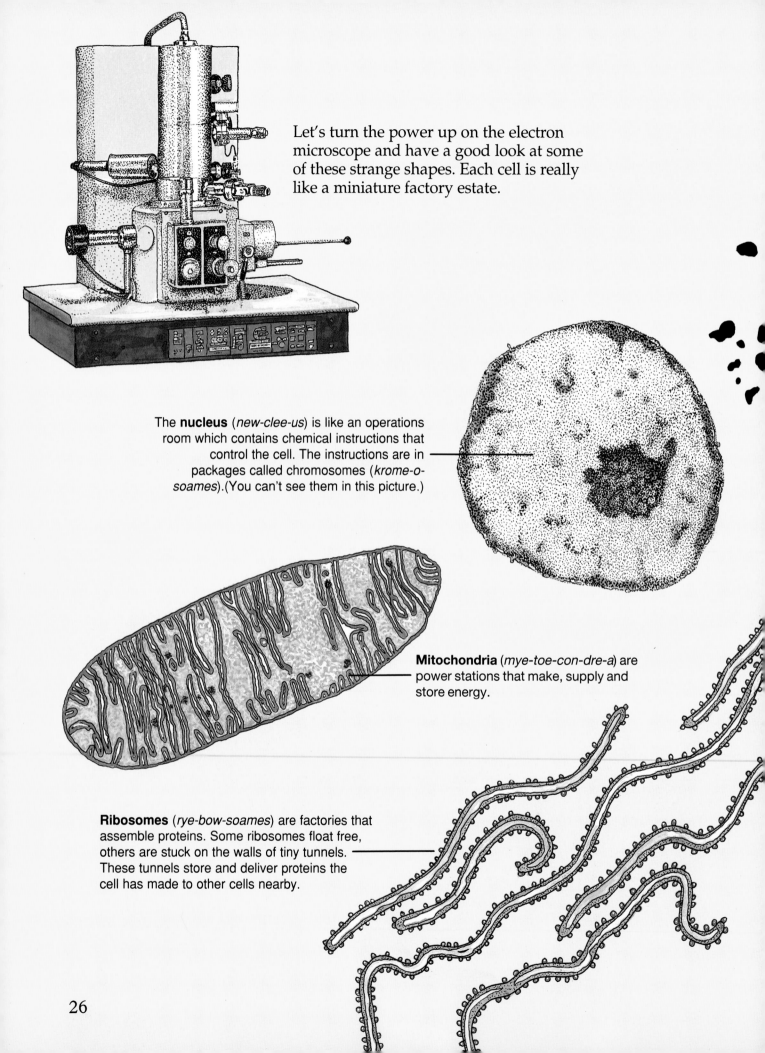

Let's turn the power up on the electron microscope and have a good look at some of these strange shapes. Each cell is really like a miniature factory estate.

The **nucleus** (*new-clee-us*) is like an operations room which contains chemical instructions that control the cell. The instructions are in packages called chromosomes (*krome-o-soames*).(You can't see them in this picture.)

Mitochondria (*mye-toe-con-dre-a*) are power stations that make, supply and store energy.

Ribosomes (*rye-bow-soames*) are factories that assemble proteins. Some ribosomes float free, others are stuck on the walls of tiny tunnels. These tunnels store and deliver proteins the cell has made to other cells nearby.

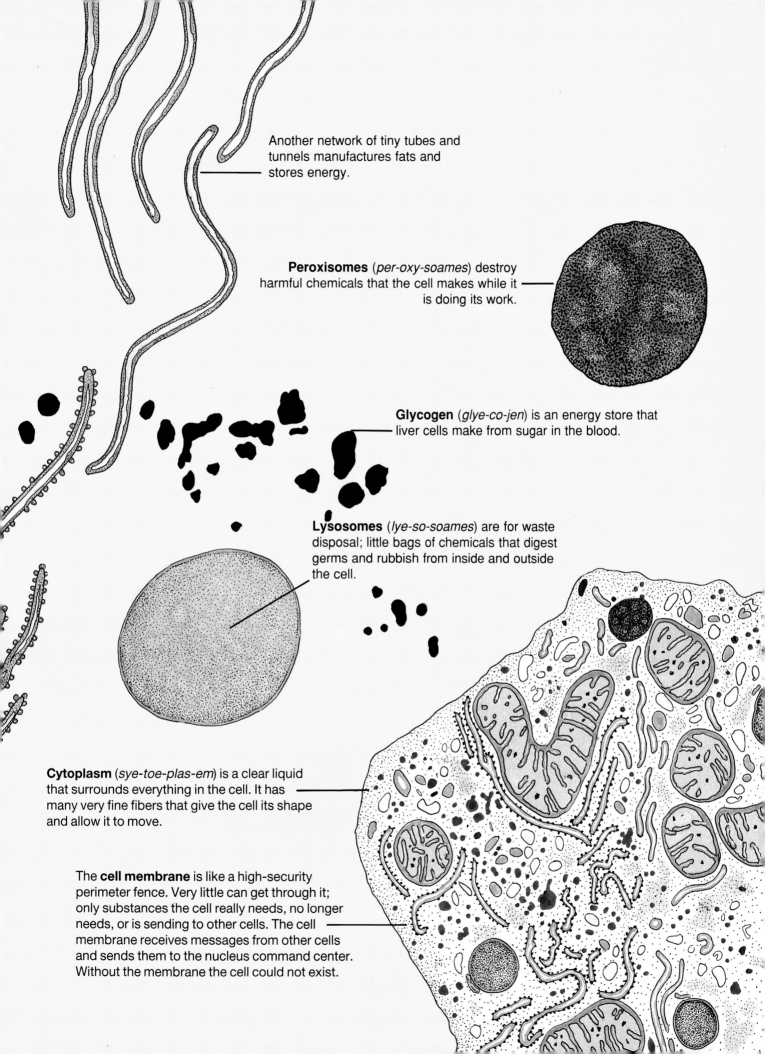

Another network of tiny tubes and tunnels manufactures fats and stores energy.

Peroxisomes (*per-oxy-soames*) destroy harmful chemicals that the cell makes while it is doing its work.

Glycogen (*glye-co-jen*) is an energy store that liver cells make from sugar in the blood.

Lysosomes (*lye-so-soames*) are for waste disposal; little bags of chemicals that digest germs and rubbish from inside and outside the cell.

Cytoplasm (*sye-toe-plas-em*) is a clear liquid that surrounds everything in the cell. It has many very fine fibers that give the cell its shape and allow it to move.

The **cell membrane** is like a high-security perimeter fence. Very little can get through it; only substances the cell really needs, no longer needs, or is sending to other cells. The cell membrane receives messages from other cells and sends them to the nucleus command center. Without the membrane the cell could not exist.

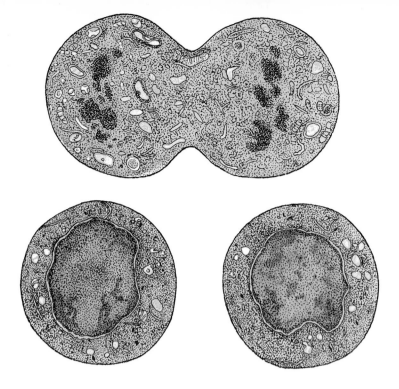

In the nucleus of every cell in your body there is an identical copy of the chemical instructions to make you, only you, and no one else but you! These chemical instructions were in the first cell that was you, and each time one of your cells divides to become two cells, these chemical instructions are copied.

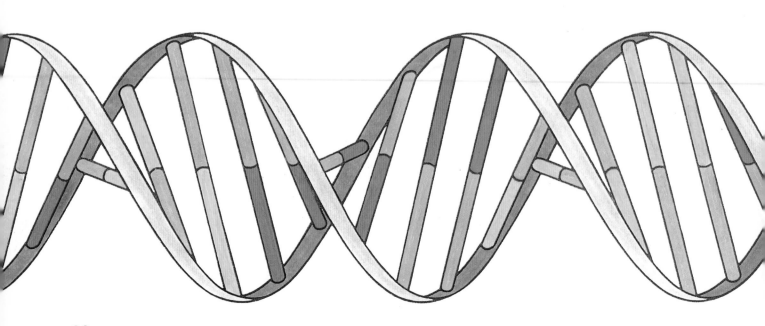

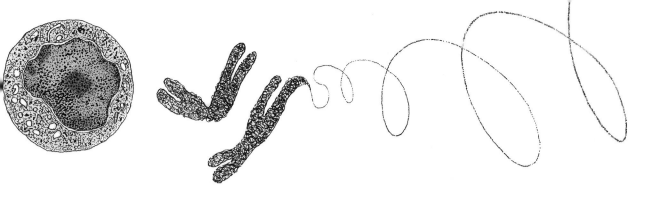

Your chemical instructions are made of a very special substance called deoxyribonucleic acid, (*dee-oxy-rye-bow-new-clee-ick acid*). What did I say? You'll be relieved to know that it is usually known as DNA.

Your DNA is coiled up in the nucleus of each of your cells in forty-six very long and very thin threads called chromosomes. The threads are so thin that you can hardly see them through a powerful electron microscope. But if you unraveled all the DNA from a single tiny cell it would stretch for five feet!
If DNA is that long, it must be very thin. In fact, you could fit about one million threads of DNA across the period at the end of this sentence.

What does DNA look like? In this diagram, we've unraveled the DNA thread from one of the chromosomes and magnified it about seventy million times. Now you can easily see one thread and discover its most important secret. Not one, but two strands make up the thread. They wind around each other so that the DNA looks like a twisting, twirling ladder. This shape is called a double helix.

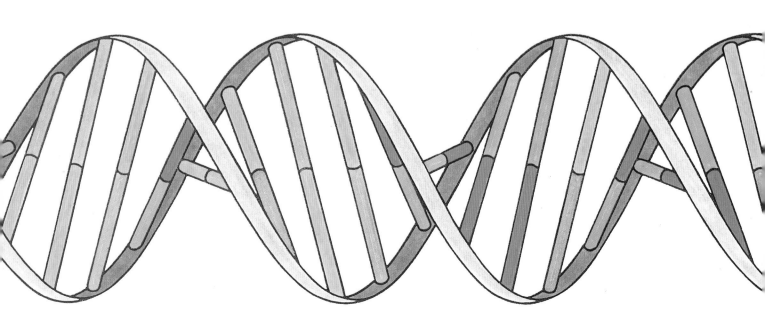

We told you that each time one of your cells divides and becomes two cells the DNA instructions are copied.
This is how it works:

1. The double helix unzips so that there are two single strands of DNA. Then each single strand becomes a pattern for another strand. The chemicals that make DNA are floating around nearby in the cell and join up in a precise order.

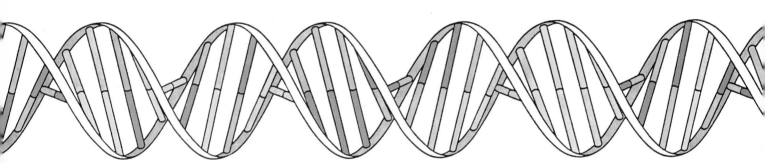

2. The four chemicals that make up your DNA thread are called –

Adenine   (*ad-en-een*)

Thymine   (*thy-meen*)

Cytosine   (*cy-toe-seen*)

Guanine   (*gwa-neen*)

We've made each of them a different color in the drawing. Adenine is red, thymine is green, cytosine is yellow and guanine is blue. The chemicals that make DNA are known by their initials **A**, **T**, **C** and **G**.

3. Can you see the order in which the chemicals are joined up? Look very carefully at the DNA that is being copied in this picture.

Chemical **A** always joins up with chemical **T**.

Chemical **T** always joins up with chemical **A**.

Chemical **C** always joins up with chemical **G**.

Chemical **G** always joins up with chemical **C**.

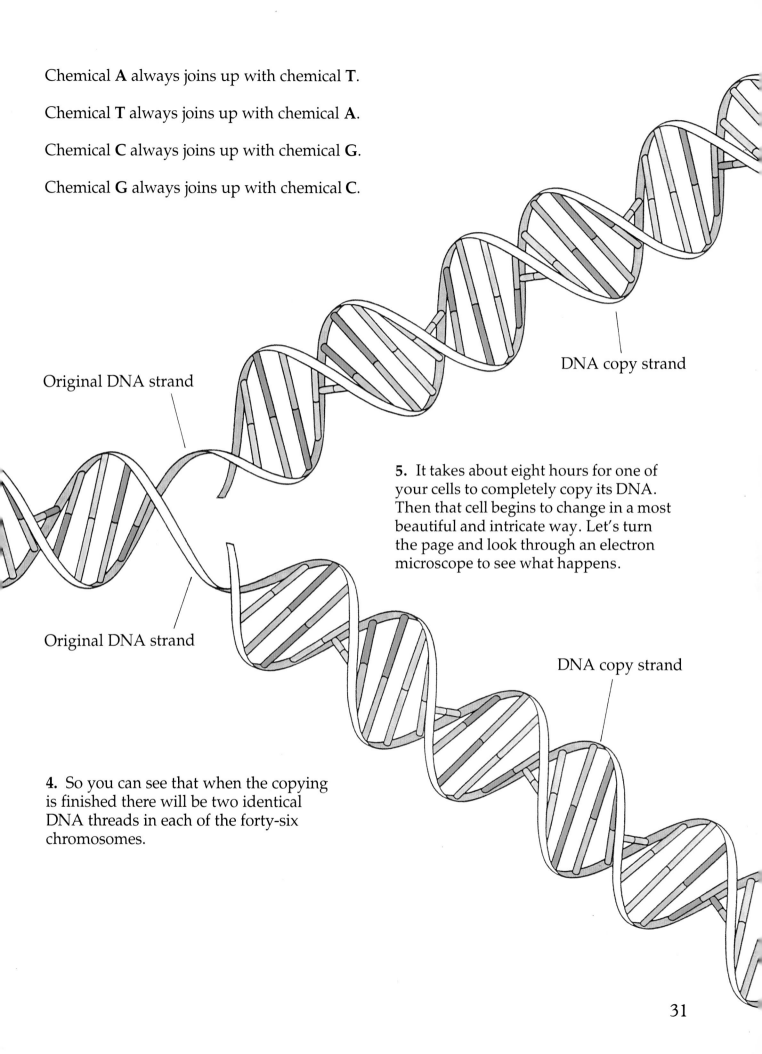

DNA copy strand

Original DNA strand

5. It takes about eight hours for one of your cells to completely copy its DNA. Then that cell begins to change in a most beautiful and intricate way. Let's turn the page and look through an electron microscope to see what happens.

Original DNA strand

DNA copy strand

4. So you can see that when the copying is finished there will be two identical DNA threads in each of the forty-six chromosomes.

31

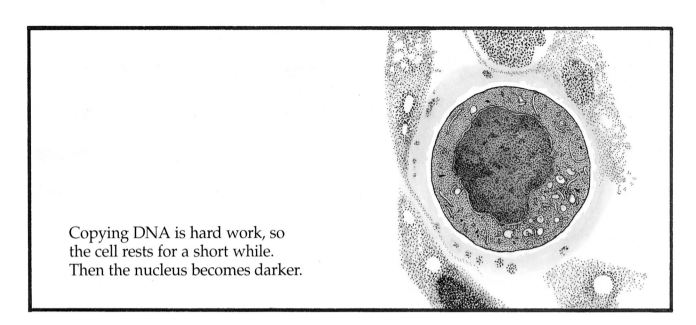

Copying DNA is hard work, so
the cell rests for a short while.
Then the nucleus becomes darker.

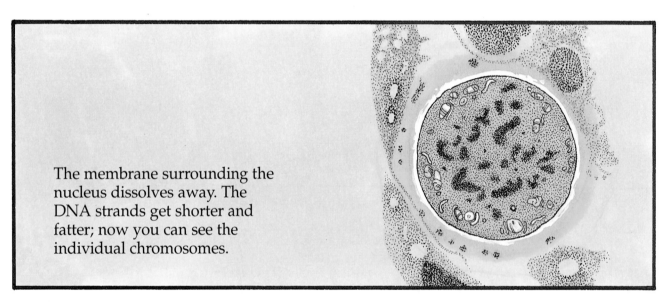

The membrane surrounding the
nucleus dissolves away. The
DNA strands get shorter and
fatter; now you can see the
individual chromosomes.

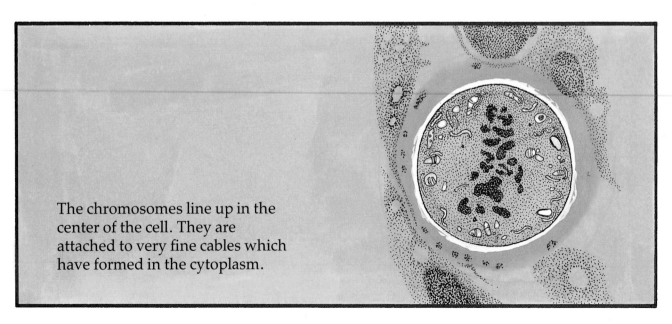

The chromosomes line up in the
center of the cell. They are
attached to very fine cables which
have formed in the cytoplasm.

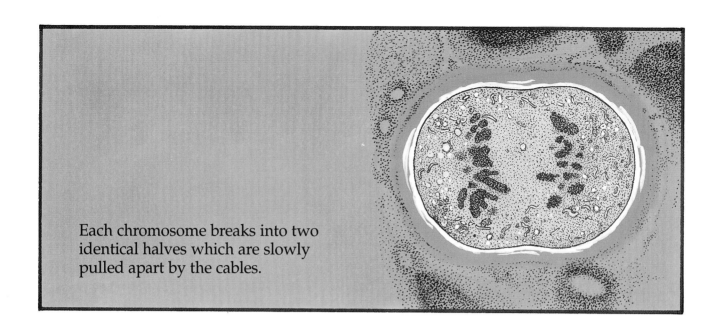

Each chromosome breaks into two identical halves which are slowly pulled apart by the cables.

Now there is one half of each chromosome at each end of the cell. The very middle of the cell becomes pinched in, as if an invisible belt is being notched tighter and tighter.

Very quickly – within ten minutes – that one cell has become two new cells, each with identical DNA instructions.

And the amazing thing is that cells from frogs, starfish, lilies and even microscopic single-celled yeasts, all divide in very much the same way.

33

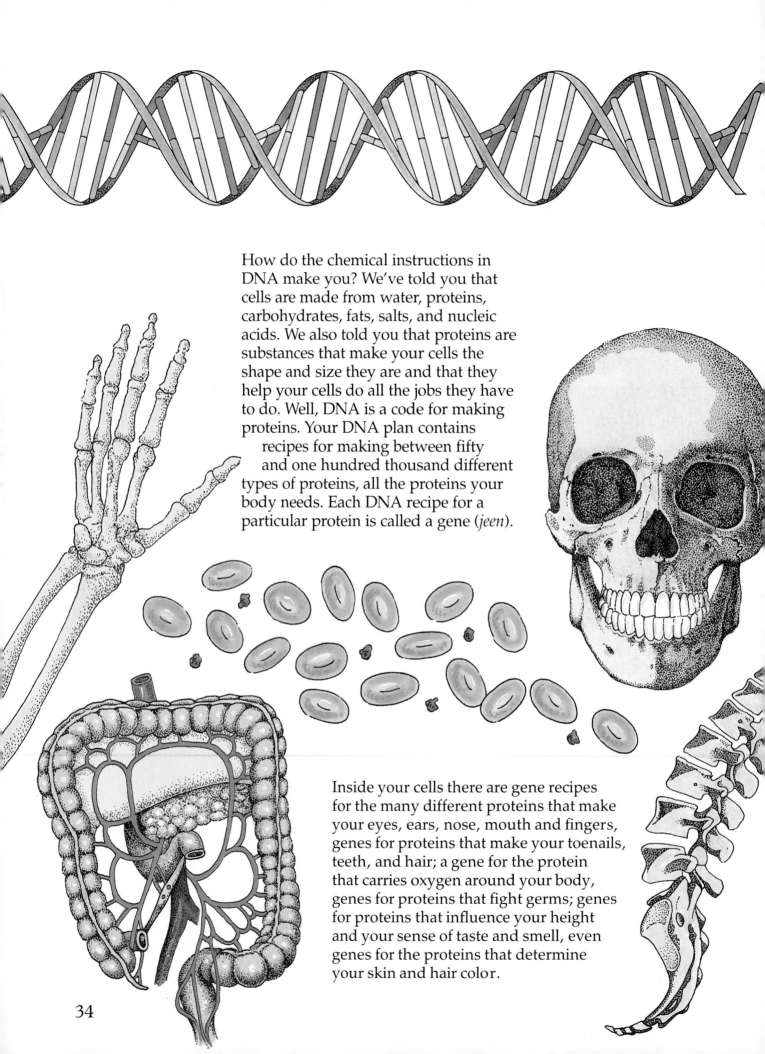

How do the chemical instructions in DNA make you? We've told you that cells are made from water, proteins, carbohydrates, fats, salts, and nucleic acids. We also told you that proteins are substances that make your cells the shape and size they are and that they help your cells do all the jobs they have to do. Well, DNA is a code for making proteins. Your DNA plan contains recipes for making between fifty and one hundred thousand different types of proteins, all the proteins your body needs. Each DNA recipe for a particular protein is called a gene (*jeen*).

Inside your cells there are gene recipes for the many different proteins that make your eyes, ears, nose, mouth and fingers, genes for proteins that make your toenails, teeth, and hair; a gene for the protein that carries oxygen around your body, genes for proteins that fight germs; genes for proteins that influence your height and your sense of taste and smell, even genes for the proteins that determine your skin and hair color.

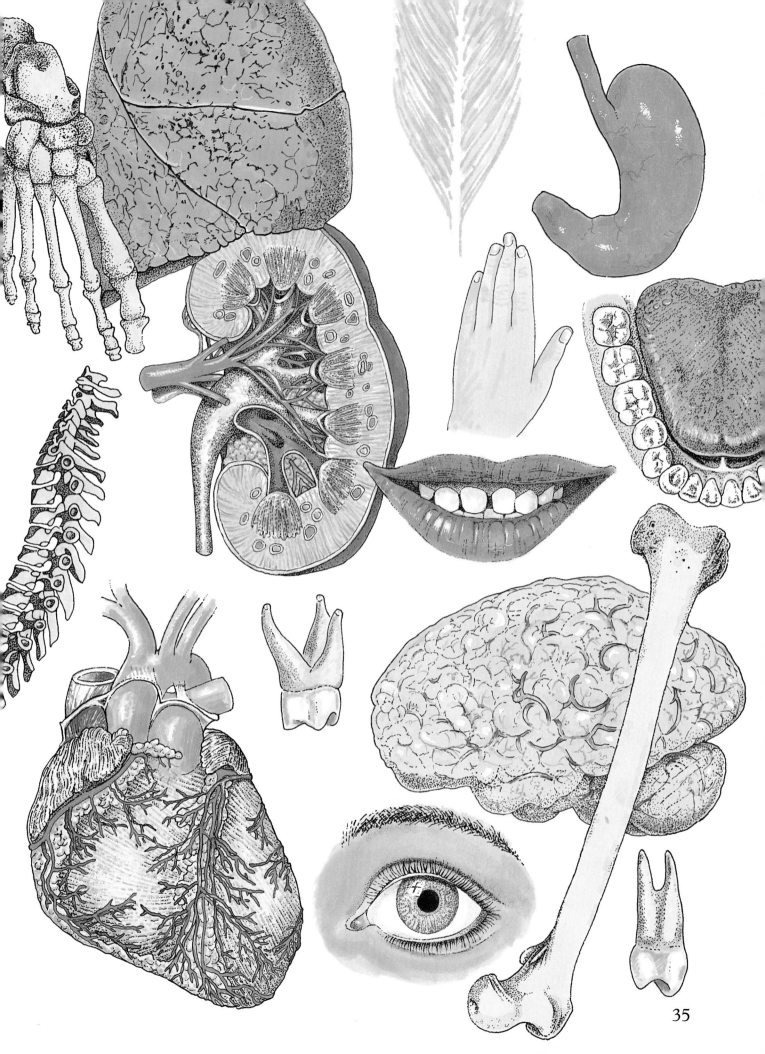

35

1. Every second of every minute of every hour of every day your cells are using gene recipes to make proteins.

1. When a protein is needed, the part of the DNA that is the gene for that protein starts to unwind from its chromosome.

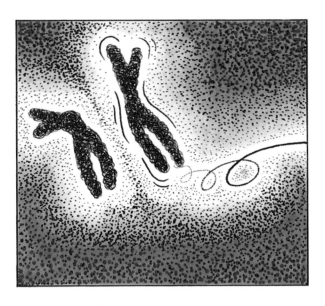

2. The gene is now ready to copy its protein recipe.

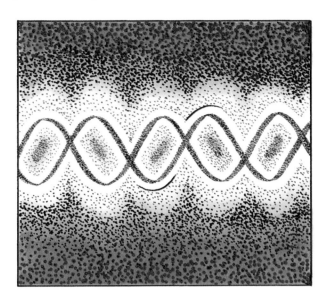

3. A copy of the gene recipe is made from one of the two DNA strands. The copy strand is called ribonucleic (*rye-bow-new-clee-ick*) acid, or RNA.

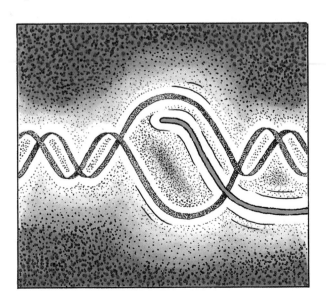

4. The RNA copy strand floats off out of the nucleus to other parts of the cell and finds some ribosomes. Ribosomes are protein-making factories.

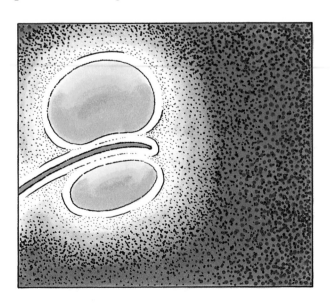

5. Proteins are made from building blocks called amino (*am-een-o*) acids that lie in the cytoplasm surrounding the ribosomes.

6. The RNA instructs the ribosomes to join up the amino acids in a precise order which is different for each protein.

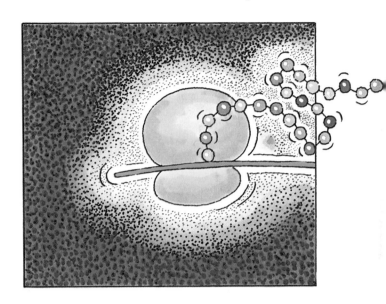

7. It takes about one minute for a ribosome to "read" the RNA. Once a complete protein is made, it leaves the ribosome and is ready to do its particular job.

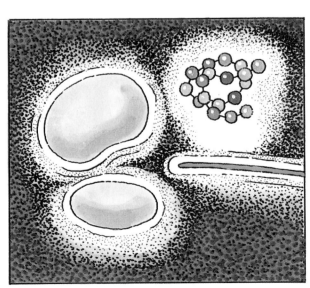

8. Proteins are also made by ribosomes attached to a special system of tunnels and passages in the cell. These are collecting channels and warehouses for proteins.

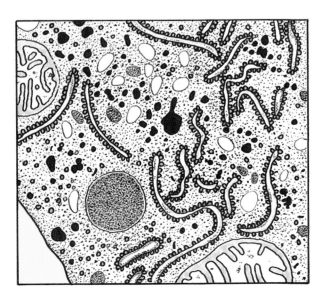

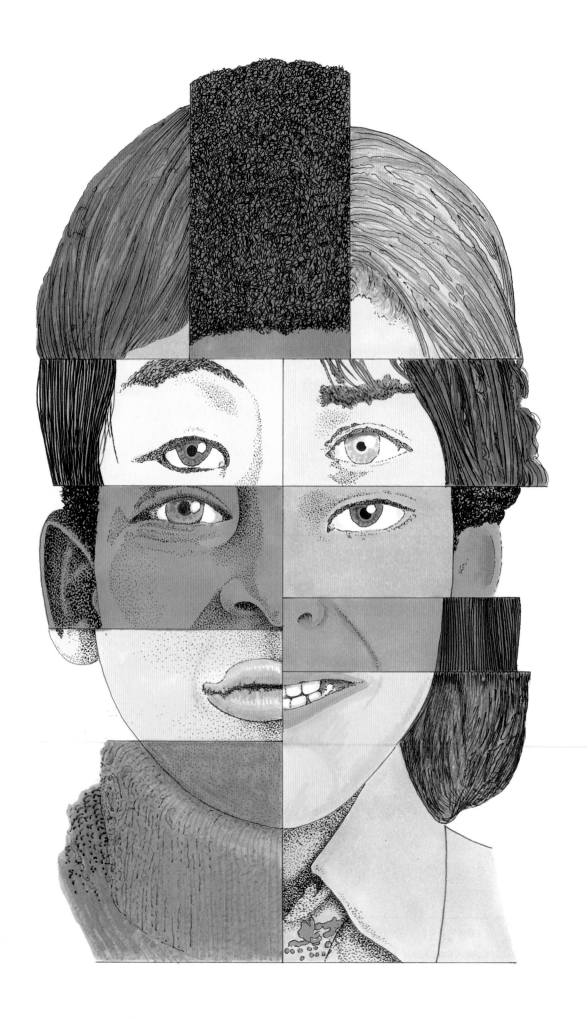

About ninety-nine and a half percent of your genes make the same proteins in every other human being in the world. But some parts of your DNA plans are unique. Your hair color genes may have recipes for blonde, brown, black or red hair. Genes for eye color may make them blue, brown, hazel, or green.

Genes for skin color may make you different shades of pink, yellow or brown. We are all slightly different from one another because some of our genes are different. That means that our cells make proteins that are slightly different from everybody else (except for identical twins who have identical DNA!).

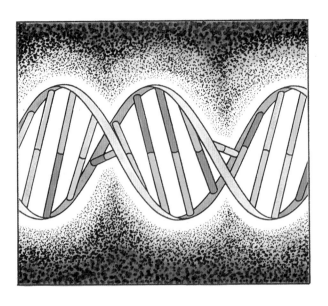

Genes are made of DNA

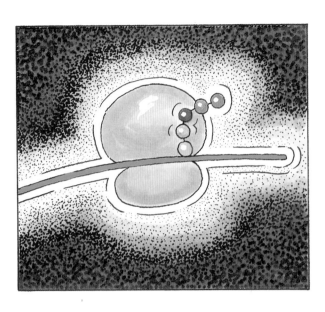

Genes are recipes for making proteins

Proteins make cells

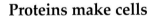

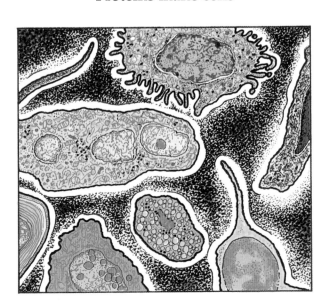

Cells make YOU!

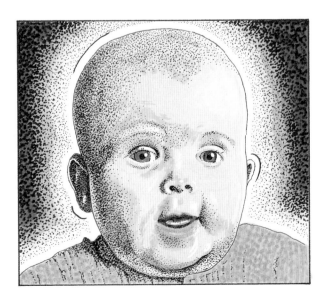

39

We've told you about your chemical plans and how they make you, but did you know that the billions of bacteria, plants and animals that live on our planet have chemical plans inside their cells as well? Now, you might think that other plants and animals would have different chemical plans to make them. You don't look much like a sparrow, a beetle, or a blade of grass – do you? But the amazing truth is that all forms of life on this planet have DNA chemical plans made of **ATCG** in their cells. They all have DNA gene recipes for proteins.

And the only reason that they are different from you is that the **ATCG**s in their DNA are lined up in a different order. This means that they have different gene recipes, and those genes make many proteins that are different from those in your cells. If you think about this for a minute, you might begin to understand how life on this planet slowly evolved over three billion years from microscopic bacteria into the living world today. Over millions of years, the DNA code that was in the first bacteria changed.

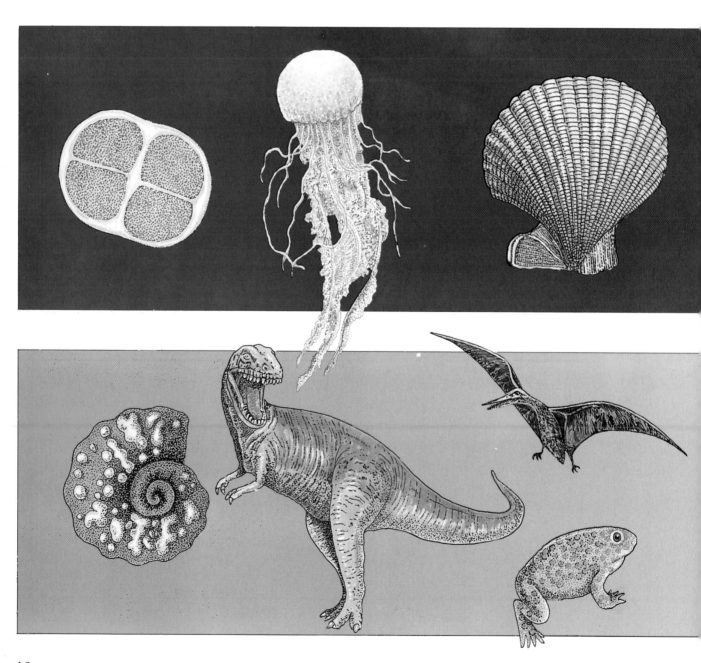

The DNA code changed because it was damaged by rays from the sun or by powerful chemicals, and because mistakes were occasionally made as the cells were copying their DNA. Changes in DNA are called mutations (*mew-tay-shons*). Mutations may mean that a cell makes different proteins. Different proteins make different life forms. Mutations allow all living creatures to change and adapt, particularly when the environment around them changes dramatically. In fact, mutations can create new species.

Mutations are the means by which life on earth has changed from a single-celled ancestor into millions of different plants and animals. You probably know that your closest living animal relatives are the apes, but did you know that ninety-eight percent of your DNA is in the same order as that of any chimpanzee you might see in a wildlife park? Only a tiny fraction of the proteins in your cells make the difference between your behavior and skills and any of the apes. And would it surprise you that one percent of your DNA is the same as that of bacteria living under your fingernails?

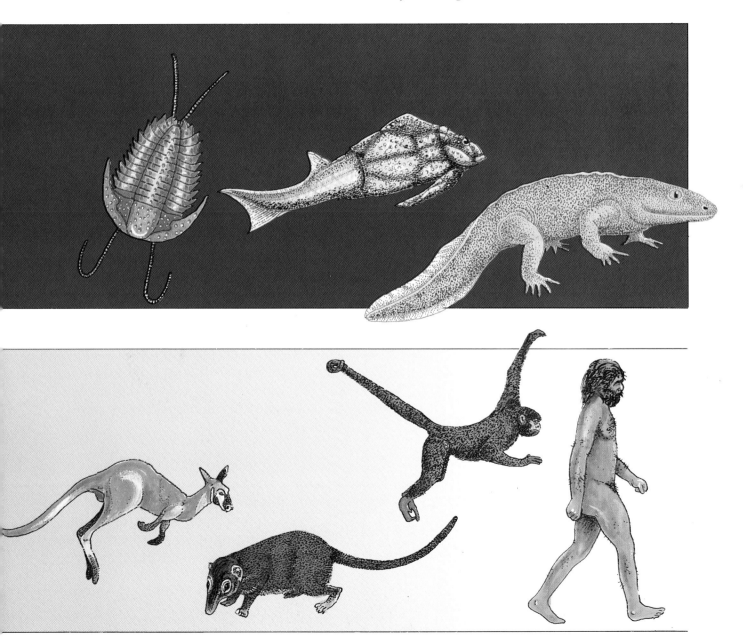

Skin Deep

So now you know what cells are, what they are made of, and what they can do. It's time to see how they work together to make YOU. We'll begin with the largest area of your body, your skin. The cells that make your skin do some very important jobs. Skin keeps the outside world our and keeps your insides in. Skin screens you against the suns's harmful rays. Skin cools you on hot days and keeps you warm when it is cold. Skin gives your body its color and hair. Skin is supple but very strong. Through your skin you can feel sharp objects, but also the softest velvet.

How do the skin cells do all this? Well, your skin has three layers. On the outside of you there is a layer of cells that are joined very tightly together. This layer is called the epidermis (*eppi-der-miss*) **(a)**. The cells in this layer make a very tough protein called keratin (*kera-tin*). Cells are continually pushed up through this layer by new cells dividing at the base. As they move up, they make more and more tough keratin proteins, until they become full of them and die. But even the dead cells have a job to do.

They stay tightly packed together and stop water and sharp objects from harming you. Eventually dead skin cells float off into the air, (that's what dust is!). It takes about four weeks for a new cell to be pushed up through the epidermis, die, protect you for a while and then float off. So, you make a new outer skin every four weeks!

The middle layer, called the dermis **(b)**, (*der-miss*) contains an intricate network of tiny tubes of blood; nerve cells that give you a sense of touch, pain and heat; cells that make hair; cells that make oil; cells that make sweat, all in a tough elastic jelly made by a protein called collagen (*coll-a-jen*).

The bottom layer (actually, there is more of this layer on your bottom) is full of fat to keep you warm. It is called the subcutaneous (*sub-kew-tain-ee-ous*) layer **(c)**.

Are you thick-skinned? In some places you are, for instance on your back and on the soles of your feet. The thinnest skin is on your eyelids. Skin can be less than four-hundredths of an inch thick, but never more than three eighths of an inch.

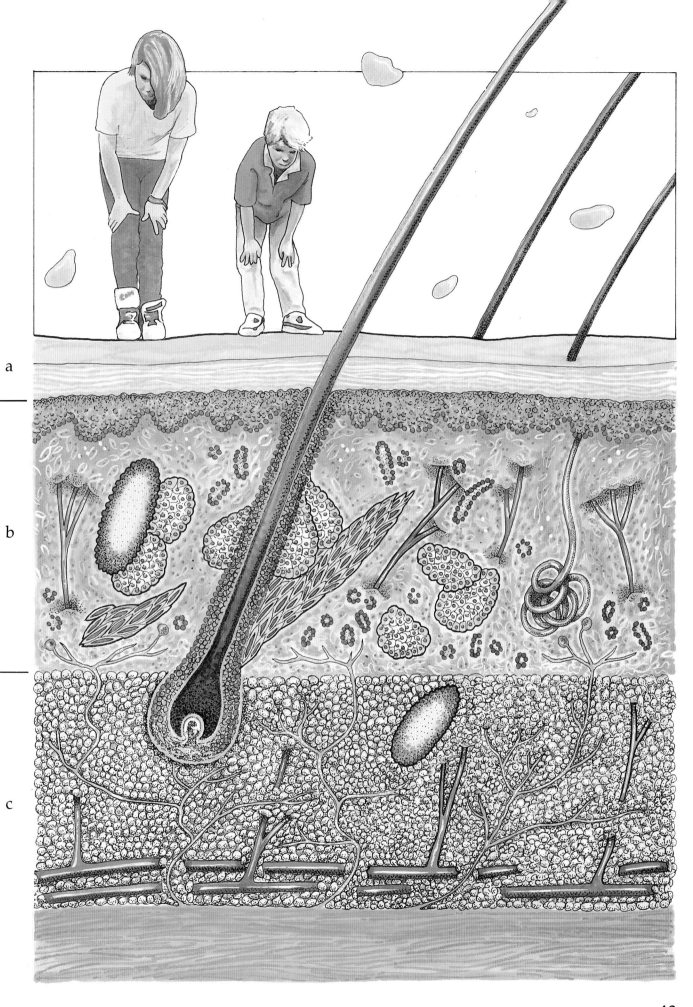

a

b

c

43

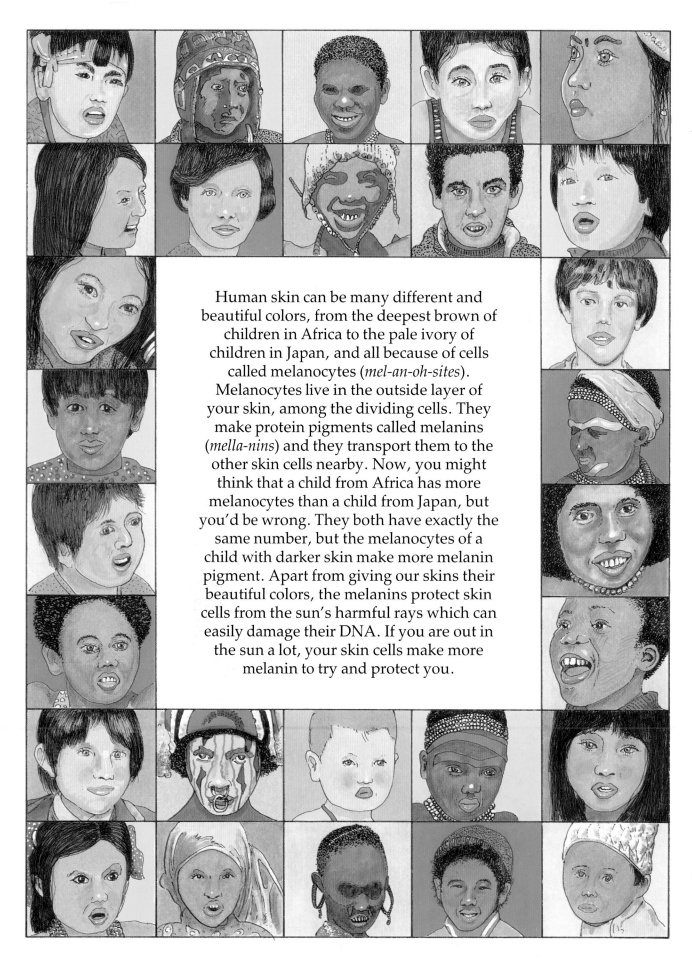

Human skin can be many different and beautiful colors, from the deepest brown of children in Africa to the pale ivory of children in Japan, and all because of cells called melanocytes (*mel-an-oh-sites*). Melanocytes live in the outside layer of your skin, among the dividing cells. They make protein pigments called melanins (*mella-nins*) and they transport them to the other skin cells nearby. Now, you might think that a child from Africa has more melanocytes than a child from Japan, but you'd be wrong. They both have exactly the same number, but the melanocytes of a child with darker skin make more melanin pigment. Apart from giving our skins their beautiful colors, the melanins protect skin cells from the sun's harmful rays which can easily damage their DNA. If you are out in the sun a lot, your skin cells make more melanin to try and protect you.

You have two million hair follicles (*fol-ik-alls*) all over your body, whether you are a boy or a girl. This is the number you were born with. Each hair follicle is a factory that makes just one hair. Did you know that there are one hundred thousand follicles making one hundred thousand hairs on your head alone? Hair is also made of that tough protein called keratin, but cells in the hair follicle make it differently from the way it is made in the cells in your skin. Instead of forming sheets to toughen your skin, keratin is made into hollow tubes of hair. Cells in the hair follicle make oils that keep your hair soft, elastic, and water repellent. Your fingernails and toenails are also made of keratin. Keratin protein is pretty versatile stuff. It is found throughout the animal kingdom. Did you know that horns, antlers, tusks, fur, hide, hooves, claws, beaks, feathers, and scales, are all made of slightly different types of keratin protein?

Over the centuries, humans have found some very important uses for keratin; leather shoes and woolly sweaters, to name but two! Unfortunately the fashion for wearing fur or the belief in the magical properties of white rhino horn are just two examples of how human misuse of animal keratin has resulted in the near extinction of many species.

Animals need their keratin more than the humans who kill them for it.

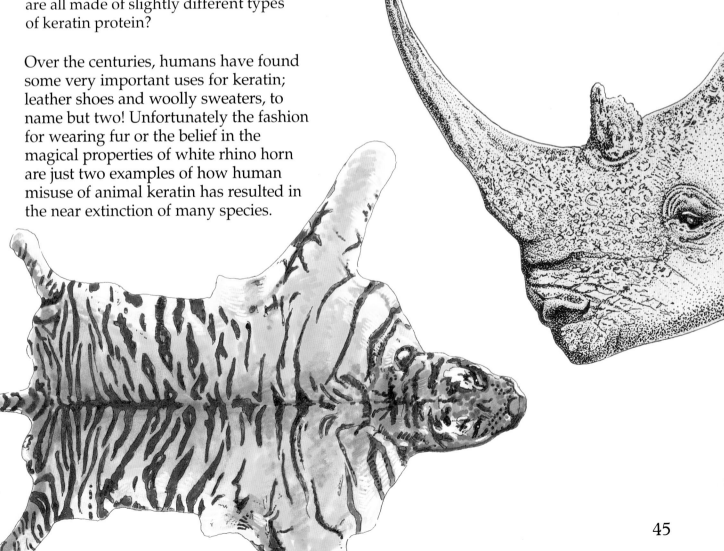

45

Blood and Gas

Think of your body as a vast city. Like all cities, its inhabitants need food supplies, communication systems, heat, energy and waste disposal. Your cells do all these jobs – and more – with just one liquid, some tubes and a very efficient pump.

Imagine that you prick your finger with a sterile needle, and squeeze a small drop of your blood onto a glass microscope slide. You spread it out a little and add a bluish pink dye that will help you see some of the cells. Place this under a microscope and you would see your blood cells – lots of them. In that small drop of blood, there would be about five million red blood cells, about ten thousand white blood cells and about two hundred and fifty thousand very small cell bits called platelets.

You would see red blood cells that carry oxygen all around your body. They are full of a special protein called hemoglobin (*heem-o-glow-bin*), that holds on to the oxygen and then releases it to cells that need it. Each red cell survives for about one hundred and twenty days (four months) in the blood. You make about ten thousand million new red blood cells every day to replace those that die.

You would see other blood cells, stained pink and blue by the dye. These are called white blood cells and they are your defender cells. They constantly patrol your blood on the lookout for germs that make you ill. If they sense trouble, they will squeeze through the tubes that carry the blood cells and … watch out germs!

You would see platelets that are tiny bits of cells with a vital job to do. They help your blood to clot so that you don't lose too much of this precious fluid when your body is damaged.

Half your blood is made from red cells, white blood cells, and platelets, the other half is made of a clear, pale yellow liquid called plasma (*plaz-ma*). Many important proteins are dissolved in plasma. Some of these proteins help your white blood cells fight germs; other proteins are hormones (*hor-moans*) that deliver chemical messages to cells around your body, and there are many, many others.

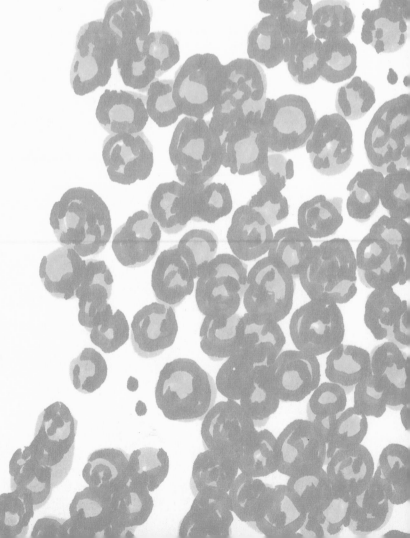

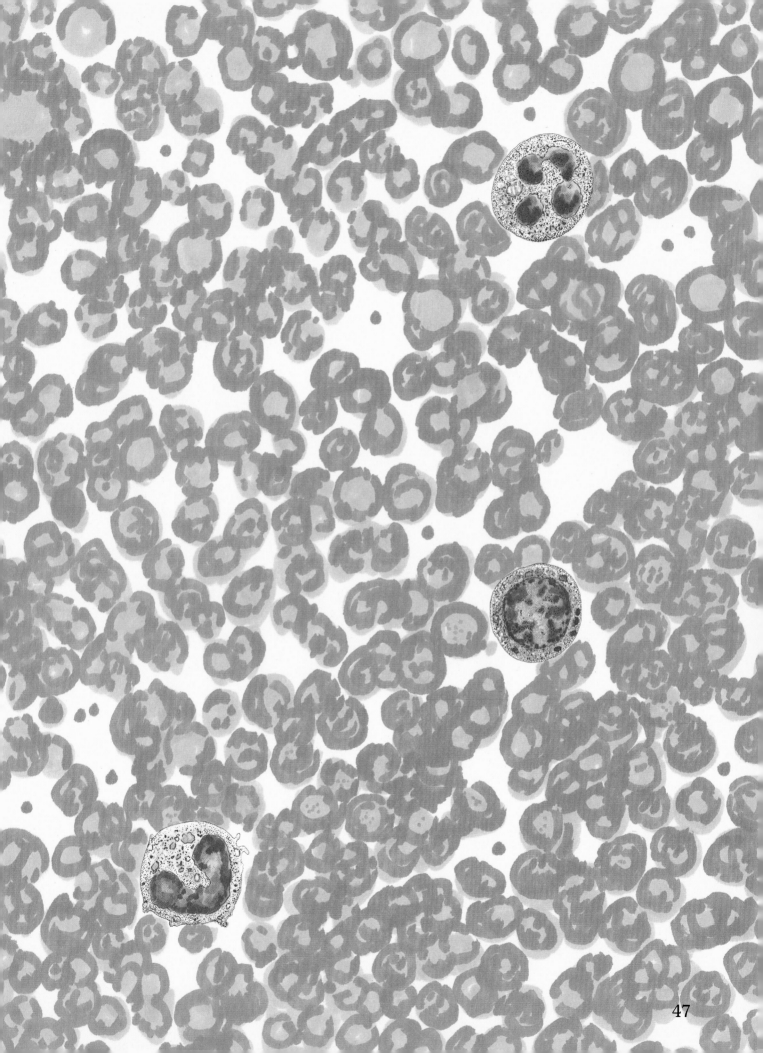

Your blood transport system works like this. Large tubes called arteries *art-er-ees*) takes blood from the left side of your heart and carry it around your body. Close to your heart, arteries have a tough outer layer, with muscle cells and elastic fibers beneath, and on the very inside, a smooth layer of flat cells which allow the blood to flow freely. Arteries branch and branch and become thinner until the tubes are just one cell wide. Blood cells have to pass through these capillaries (*cap-ill-a-rees*), in single file. Oxygen, food and liquid pass through the capillaries to cells in need, and waste passes back. The capillaries get thicker and wider and join up to form veins (*vanes*) which carry blood back to the right side of the heart. The veins have special valves which make sure blood doesn't flow backwards. Blood is now pumped to your lungs to collect oxygen and returns to the left side of the heart to go around the body again. The whole journey takes only one minute!

Every day about three quarts of fluid is lost from capillaries into spaces between cells. This is collected up by tubes of the lymphatic (*lim-fat-ick*) system. The fluid, called lymph (*limf*), and fat from the intestines travels through these tubes back to the blood via veins in your chest. The lymphatic system also provides a home and transport system for defender cells. Lymph passes through lymph nodes which are packed with defender cells on the lookout for germs. Your tonsils (if you still have them!) are lymph nodes.

48

This shows a slice of a small artery (actual size about twelve thousandths of an inch). Lining cells are surmounted by elastic tissue and smooth muscle.

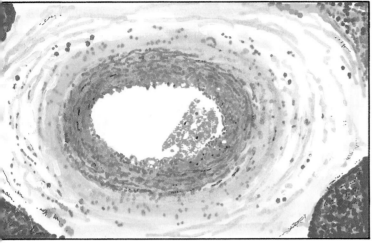

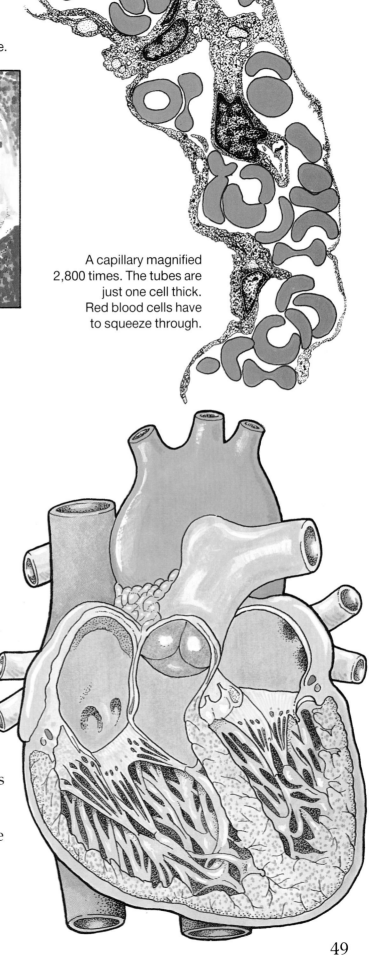

A capillary magnified 2,800 times. The tubes are just one cell thick. Red blood cells have to squeeze through.

Clench your fist – your heart is about that size: a very efficient muscular pump. A pump that can go on working every second for over one hundred years! Your heart has a thin layer of smooth cells on the inside, and then muscle, nerves, a fibrous protein called collagen, elastic tissues and fat cells. The muscle cells of the heart are very special, you don't find cells like them anywhere else in your body. They have lots of mitochondria power stations inside them because they need lots of energy to do their work. The muscle cells on the left side have to pump blood all around your body, and then when it returns, the right side pumps it to your lungs.

Each side of the heart has two chambers: The auricles (*orr-ick-alls*) where blood is collected and ventricles (*ven-trick-alls*) which have stronger muscles to pump blood out of the heart. The beating sound you can hear if you put your ear to someone's chest is made by the valves shutting, first the valves between the auricles and the ventricles, second the valves between the ventricles and the arteries.

49

Why is it so important that blood goes to your lungs? Because of a gas called oxygen. Very few cells in your body can survive without oxygen for more than a few minutes. Cells use oxygen and carbohydrates to make energy.

Lungs are the spongiest part of your body, because they contain three hundred million tiny air sacs, each just a single cell thick. You breathe air containing oxygen through your nose and mouth into a big thick muscular tube called the trachea (*tray-kee-uh*), which branches into two tubes, called bronchi (*bron-kee*), one to each of your lungs. Each tube then branches again and again. The lining cells of these tubes have tiny hairs that waft away the dirt and germs that you breath in.

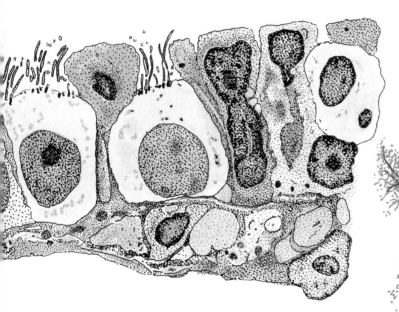

The tubes get finer and finer and end in lots of tiny little air sacs called alveoli (*al-vee-oh-lie*). If you were to spread all three hundred million of them out they would cover an area the size of a tennis court, an enormous area for absorbing oxygen! Capillaries lie close to the air sacs. There are more capillaries in your lungs than anywhere else in your body. The oxygen in your lungs is taken up by red blood cells in the capillaries.

50

But your lungs don't just absorb oxygen, they also take away a very poisonous gas called carbon dioxide (*car-bon die-ox-ide*). Your body is a bit like a car. When a car uses oxygen to burn fuel for energy, carbon dioxide is made. Carbon dioxide passes from the capillaries to your lungs through the tubes and out into the air. You could say that your bronchi are like car exhaust pipes!

Lungs are protected by your rib cage. Underneath there is a very powerful muscle that almost divides your body in

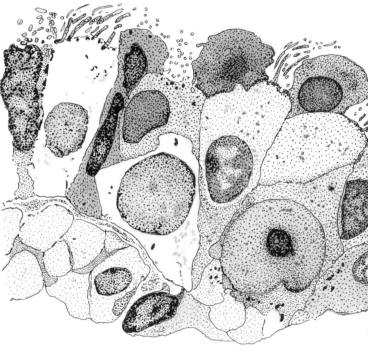

half, the diaphragm (*die-a-fram*). This helps you breathe. Breathe in: your diaphragm contracts and air is drawn into your lungs. Breathe out: your diaphragm relaxes and air is forced out through your nose. You breathe twelve to twenty times a minute, twenty-four hours of the day all of your life.

On these pages you can see some of the cells that line your breathing tubes magnified about 2,000 times.

51

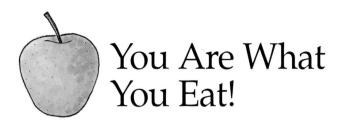

You Are What You Eat!

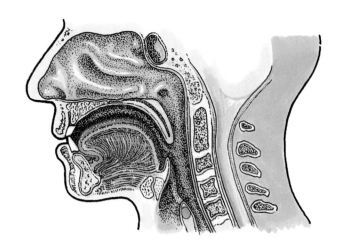

You know that your cells use proteins, fats, carbohydrates, water, nucleic acids, vitamins and tiny amounts of metals like iron and zinc, to make your body. And that is what you eat, in all about sixty-five thousand pounds during your whole life!

Your digestive system is an incredible food processor, a tube that churns and turns food into substances that your cells can use. You decide what to put in your mouth and whether to chew and swallow it, but after that the tube takes over. The first part, called the esophagus (*ee-sof-ag-us*), is short, thick and muscular. It pushes down the food, mixed with saliva, even if you are eating up-side down!

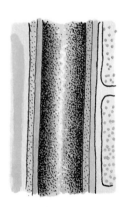

Then the tube leads into a wide cavern, a sagging J-shaped bag, your stomach. Here food is churned and mixed with acid to kill off dangerous germs you might have eaten; and enzymes (*en-zimes*) from the stomach and from the saliva begin to break the food down into more basic chemicals.

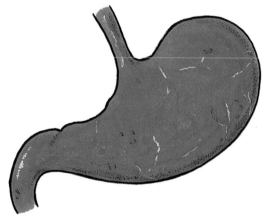

The soupy, gloppy food enters the next part of the tube, the small intestine, all twenty feet of it coiled up inside you like a hose pipe. The walls are made of millions of tiny folds that make an enormous surface for absorbing food. More and more enzymes are squirted in. Proteins, fats and carbohydrates are turned into even more basic chemicals.

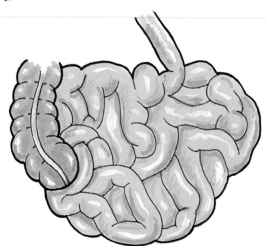

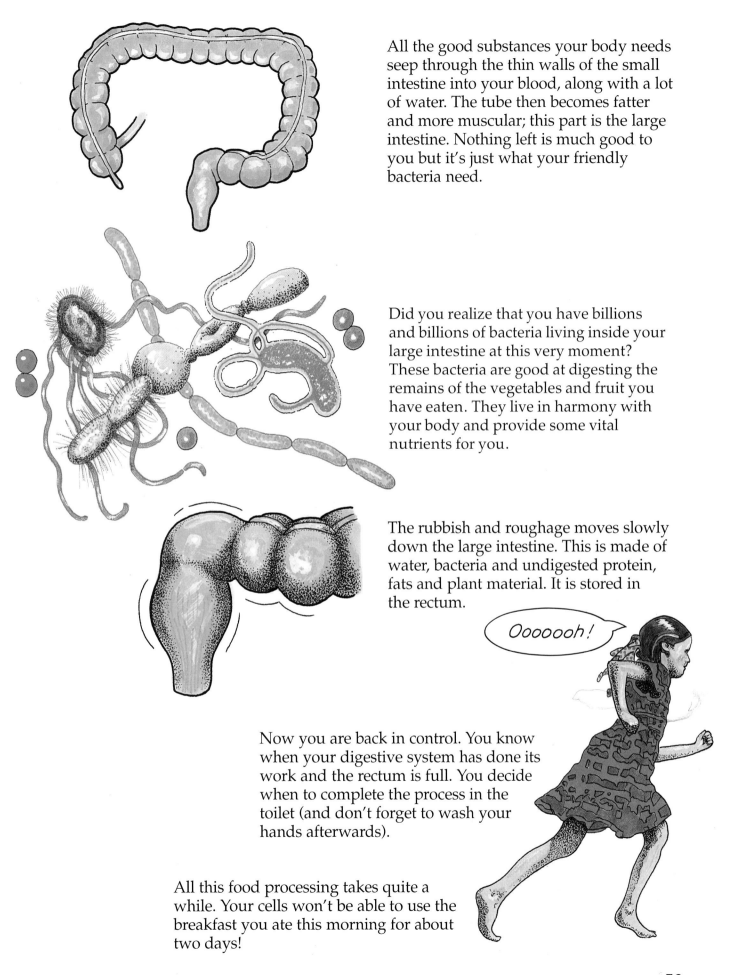

All the good substances your body needs seep through the thin walls of the small intestine into your blood, along with a lot of water. The tube then becomes fatter and more muscular; this part is the large intestine. Nothing left is much good to you but it's just what your friendly bacteria need.

Did you realize that you have billions and billions of bacteria living inside your large intestine at this very moment? These bacteria are good at digesting the remains of the vegetables and fruit you have eaten. They live in harmony with your body and provide some vital nutrients for you.

The rubbish and roughage moves slowly down the large intestine. This is made of water, bacteria and undigested protein, fats and plant material. It is stored in the rectum.

Oooooh!

Now you are back in control. You know when your digestive system has done its work and the rectum is full. You decide when to complete the process in the toilet (and don't forget to wash your hands afterwards).

All this food processing takes quite a while. Your cells won't be able to use the breakfast you ate this morning for about two days!

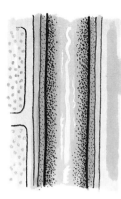

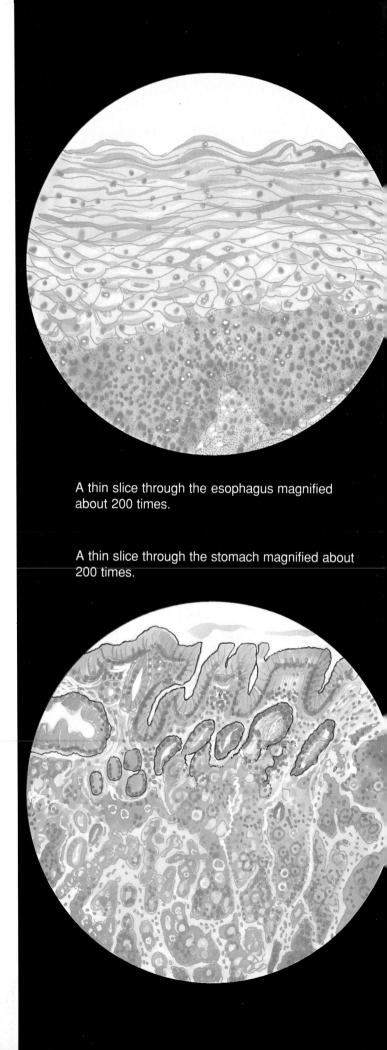

A wonderful collection of cells makes up your digestion tube. Muscle cells are outside, then there is a layer of blood vessels, defender cells, and enzyme-making cells. On the very inside, close to the food, are lining cells. These are replaced every six days because of all the wear and tear they suffer. This is what a tiny slice of your esophagus looks like through an ordinary microscope.

A thin slice through the esophagus magnified about 200 times.

A thin slice through the stomach magnified about 200 times.

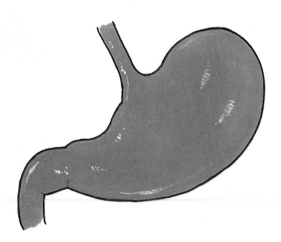

In these pictures it is very difficult to see the single cells because the microscope has only magnified them about two hundred times. In fact, there are over one thousand cells in each of the drawings. This is a tiny slice of your stomach. There are some amazing cells here that make an acid powerful enough to kill living cells! Other cells make enzymes that start digestion.

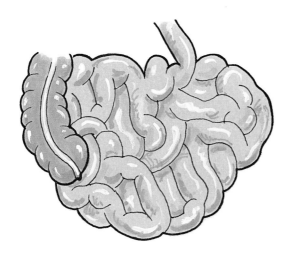

In the small intestine, proteins become amino acids, fats turn into tiny droplets, and carbohydrates are digested into simple sugars. The cells of the small intestine absorb all this. Not only are they arranged in folds, but the tip of each cell that touches the digested food is also in folds! If you flattened it out, your small intestine would have the same area as a table tennis table.

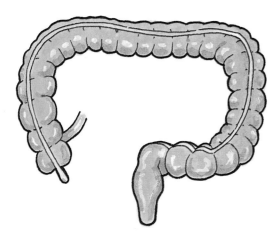

So, the cells of your digestive tube make some very interesting patterns. But in your body the cells are really grey and grainy. We added a pink dye so that you could see the way they work together easily. This is what a tiny slice of your large intestine looks like. It is tough, strong and muscular. The cells here absorb water and make a gloppy protein called mucus (*mew-cuss*) to help the undigested food move along.

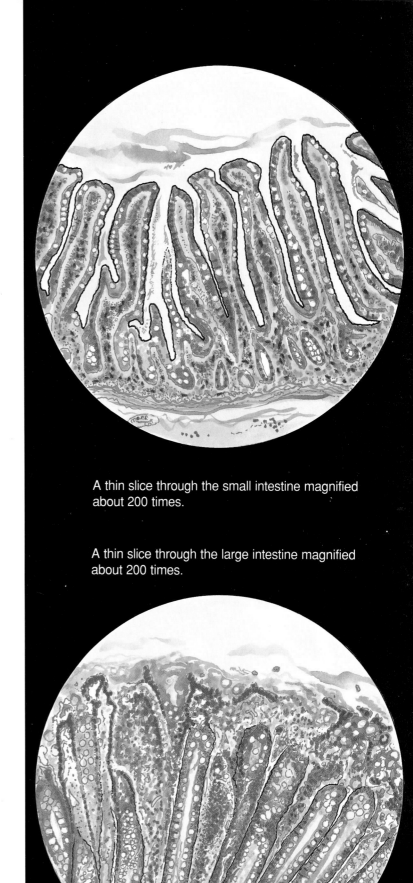

A thin slice through the small intestine magnified about 200 times.

A thin slice through the large intestine magnified about 200 times.

Your blood does not carry all this digested food straight to your cells. Blocking the path of every drop of blood that leaves your intestines is your liver. Tucked underneath the diaphragm and protected by your rib cage, the liver is the largest organ inside your body and you cannot live without it. If blood went straight round your body without being filtered through your liver, you would soon become extremely ill. This is because your liver is an enormous, versatile and complicated chemical treatment plant. It takes substances from the blood and turns them into the right foods for your cells. It also renders many poisonous substances harmless.

Blood from the intestines flows very rapidly through your liver. The large blood vessels in the liver branch many times into tiny thin tubes that leak out their contents to nearby liver cells called hepatocytes (*hep-at-o-sites*). These are large cells that are arranged in cords around the leaky blood vessels. Among them are cells called macrophages (*mac-ro-fay-jes*) that gobble up any rubbish in the blood.

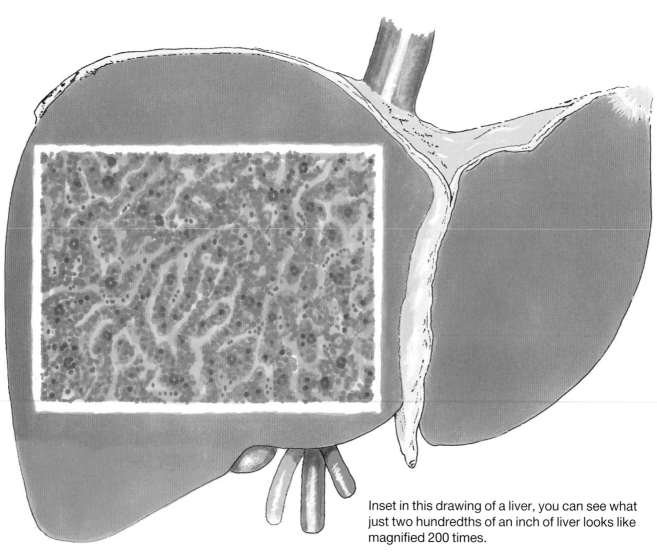

Inset in this drawing of a liver, you can see what just two hundredths of an inch of liver looks like magnified 200 times.

The cells in your liver are pretty amazing cells by any standards. These are just some of the jobs they can do:

a. Make bile that helps you digest fat.
b. Break down alcohol so it is less harmful.
c. Clear the blood of bacteria from the intestines.
d. Turn food into what your body really needs or store it for a hungry day.
e. Make many poisons harmless.
f. Recycle dead and dying blood cells.

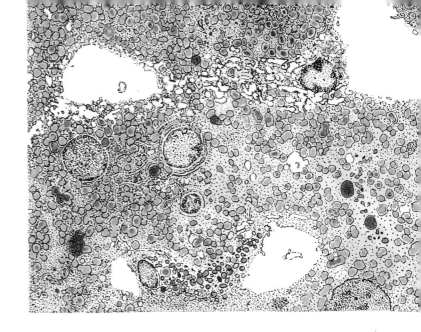

This area of the liver has been magnified about 2,000 times using an electron microscope.

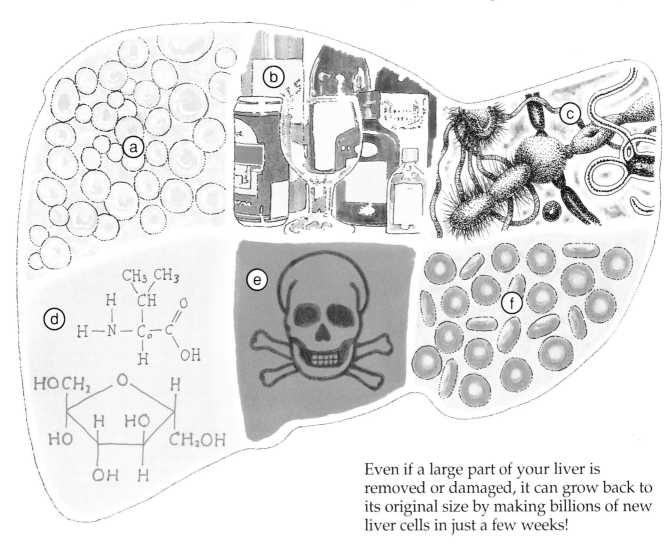

Even if a large part of your liver is removed or damaged, it can grow back to its original size by making billions of new liver cells in just a few weeks!

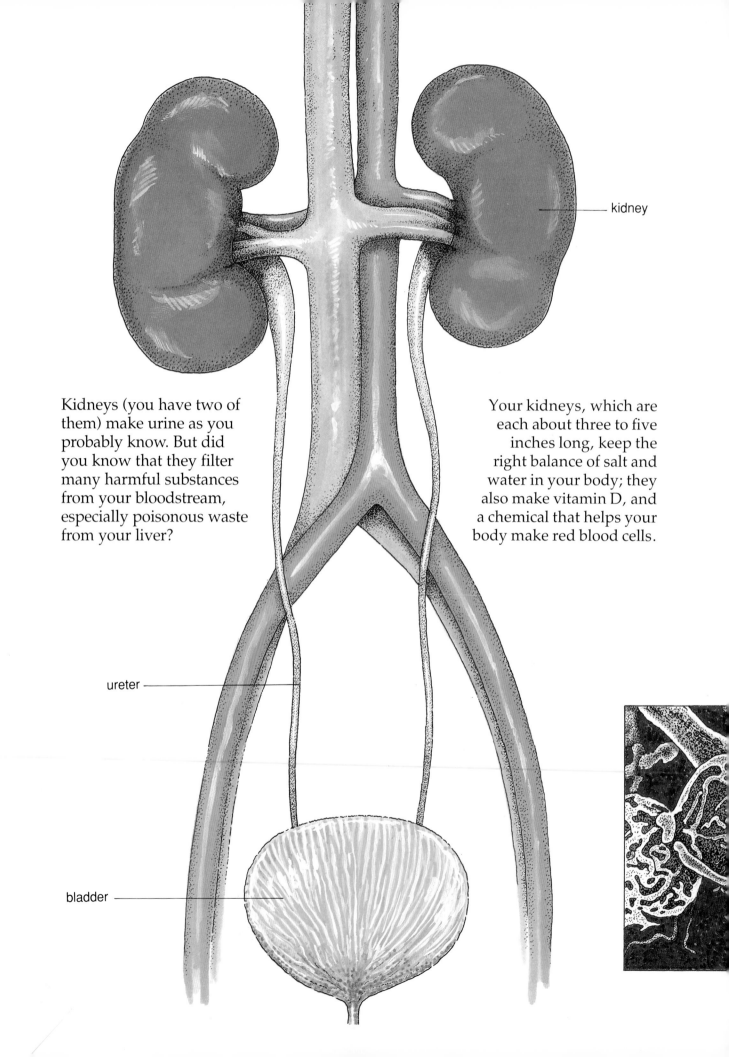

kidney

Kidneys (you have two of them) make urine as you probably know. But did you know that they filter many harmful substances from your bloodstream, especially poisonous waste from your liver?

Your kidneys, which are each about three to five inches long, keep the right balance of salt and water in your body; they also make vitamin D, and a chemical that helps your body make red blood cells.

ureter

bladder

Every day thirty-eight quarts of blood are filtered by your kidneys, but they only make one or two quarts of urine. This is what happens. The blood vessels entering the kidney turn into tiny balls of looping and twisting tubes with minute holes in them. They are called glomeruli (*glom-e-rule-aye*). (You can see what they look like in the drawing at the bottom of this page.) Water and many other substances leak out of the glomeruli. This is collected in tubes called nephrons (*nef-rons*). You have about one million of these!

As this fluid trickles through the nephrons, the cells there take back all the good things your body needs and leave the harmful waste products, plus a bit of water. This fluid passes from each kidney down two tubes called the ureters (*you-reet-ers*) to the bladder. The bladder is a sac made of muscles and nerves that are sensitive to stretching. When the bladder has about seven ounces of urine in it, the stretch receptors send messages to the brain…

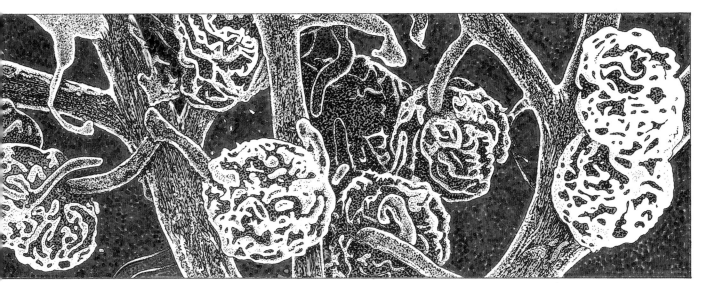

Power Beneath Your Skin

Your skeleton is made from about two hundred and ten bones. Bones that support you, protect you, move you and make your shape. But if you think that your bones are dry and dead like a skeleton in a museum, you are wrong. Your bones are very much alive. They are supplied with many blood vessels and nerves, and they are forever changing shape and size, even when you have stopped growing. Bone is made by cells called osteo**blasts** (*os-tee-o-blasts*) **(a)**, kept healthy by cells called osteo**cytes** (*os-tee-o-sites*) **(b)**, and shaped and repaired by really giant cells called osteo**clasts** (*os-tee-o-clasts*) **(c)**. Bone is hard because the

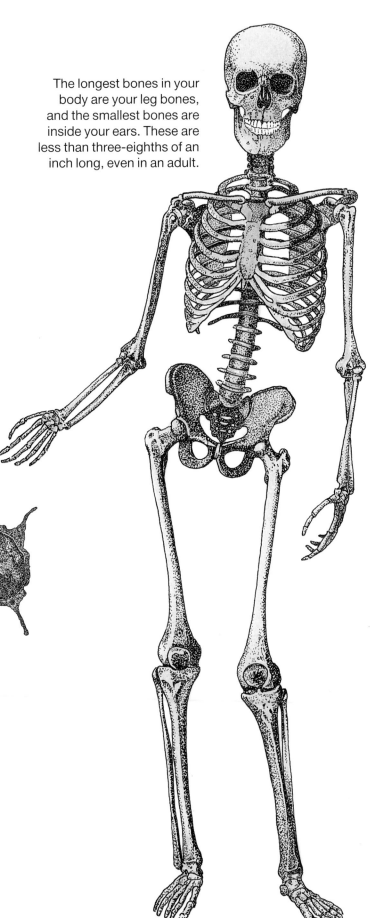

The longest bones in your body are your leg bones, and the smallest bones are inside your ears. These are less than three-eighths of an inch long, even in an adult.

a

b

c

osteoblasts make a protein called collagen and surround themselves with it. Minerals like calcium and phosphorus form hard crystals on this protein scaffolding.

That mixture sets as hard as concrete, but most of your bones have soft centers called bone marrow. Bone marrow is an incredibly busy and efficient blood cell factory. Every minute, bone marrow makes about one hundred and fifty million red blood cells to replace those that die, and every day it has to replace one billion defender white blood cells!

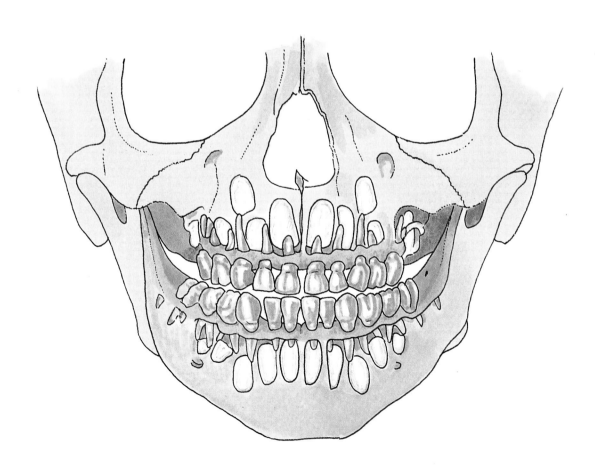

Bones are not the hardest part of your body: your teeth are! You can see the crown of each tooth in the mirror, but a longer part, called the root, goes deep into your jaw.

Inside each tooth is the pulp, made of minute blood vessels, nerves and cells called fibroblasts (*fye-bro-blasts*). Around this is a very hard layer called dentine then a layer of enamel, the hardest substance in your body. Like bone, dentine and enamel are made of crystals of calcium and phosphorus, laid around a scaffolding of protein. Dentine is made by cells called odontoblasts (*o-don-toe-blasts* (and enamel is made by ameloblasts (*am-ee-low-blasts*).

As you have probably discovered, you have two sets of teeth in your life: twenty baby teeth, that are replaced by thirty-two permanent teeth which start growing when you are about six years old. No one knows what triggers a permanent tooth to start growing in its bony space deep in your jaw.

As the new tooth expands, osteoclast cells eat away the bone in the jaw and the new tooth begins pressing on the old one. Osteoclast cells dissolve away the root and pulp of the baby tooth, until all that is left is the crown attached to your gum. A quick wiggle, and you can put it under your pillow for the tooth fairy!

The problem is that your teeth, unlike many other parts of your body, cannot repair themselves easily when they get damaged, and they often get damaged. This is because teeth are covered by a jelly-like layer of food and bacteria. The bacteria live on carbohydrates that you eat. Their favorite food is sugar. As they eat up the sugar, they make powerful acids that dissolve the enamel and dentine right through to the pulp, and that hurts! So don't give those bacteria a chance. Cut out sugary foods and drinks and brush your teeth regularly, day and night.

Sit very still for a moment – try not to move your body at all. You can't; it's impossible. Your heart is beating, intestines pumping, blood vessels pulsating, eyelids blinking, chest rising and falling – and all because your muscles are constantly working.

The drawings on this page are of your muscle cells magnified about two hundred times. At the top are your cardiac (*car-dee-ack*) muscles, which work very hard in your heart.

The next drawing shows your smooth muscles which work in your blood vessels, intestines, hair follicles and in your bladder. Cardiac and smooth muscles work without your ever having to think about them.

But you do control the third type of muscle. This is shown in the bottom drawing and is called striped or voluntary muscle. There are about six hundred and fifty of these muscles anchored to your bones. They make up over forty percent of your body weight.

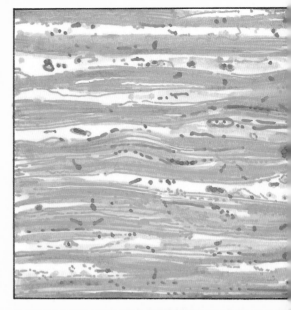

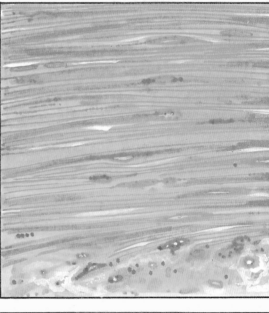

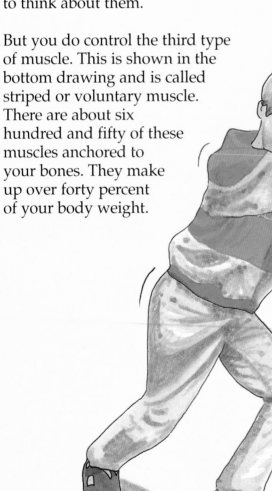

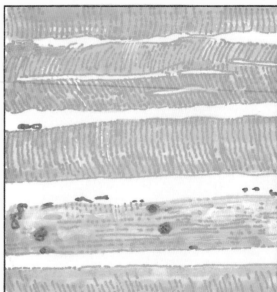

62

Muscles move your body, but they also make a lot of heat and they maintain your body in a stable position. They do all this by changing shape, becoming shorter and fatter. Muscles are made of hundreds or thousands of very long cylinder-shaped cells joined together. All muscle cells contain two slick proteins called actin (*act-in*) and myosin (*my-oh-sin*). Muscles get shorter and fatter because the actin and myosin proteins slide across each other making the muscles smaller. Muscles are very well supplied with blood vessels and nerves. Nerves from the brain carry the electrical messages that make muscles move.

I wonder why ?

Magothy River Middle School
241 Peninsula Farm Road
Arnold, MD 21012

Did you know that muscles can only pull your bones – they can't push them? Your bones move because many muscles work in pairs. As one muscle contracts and gets shorter, another relaxes and becomes longer and thinner. The easiest place to see this working is your arms. Put this book down.
Now pick it up again.
As you put the book down, a muscle at the back of your arm, called the triceps, contracted and got smaller. At exactly the same time, the muscle at the front of your arm, called the biceps, relaxed and got larger. So your arm straightened.
When you picked the book up again, the biceps contracted and the triceps relaxed. Your arm and the book moved up.

Other muscles help to steady each movement and make sure that the most important moving muscles work efficiently. For instance: Flex your wrist, and try to make a really strong fist. Difficult, isn't it?

Now straighten out your hand from your wrist – it's much easier to make a fist now because the muscles of your wrist help the muscles in your fingers.

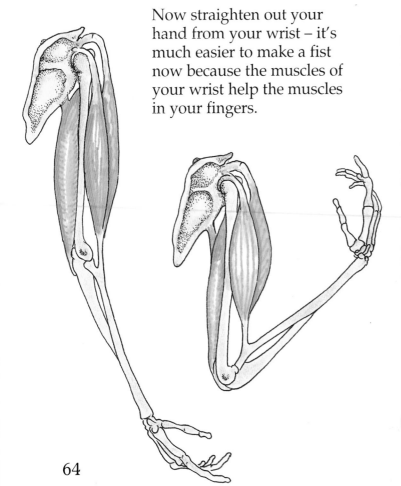

64

Tendons are like strong ropes that join muscles to bones. They have to be strong to control some of your most powerful muscles. Some tendons are very close to the surface of your skin. The hamstring tendon helps your knee to bend. Can you feel it at the back of your knee?

Bones must be joined together strongly to keep you from falling apart, but your body is quite flexible. Bones are too rigid to bend at all, but they can move where they meet other bones. This place where two bones meet is called a joint. You also find cartilage in joints. This is less rigid than bone, it prevents friction and acts as a shock absorber. Joints protect the ends of bones and allow all kinds of different movements because of some very clever engineering.

Humans have invented hinges, pivots, and joints to help many different machines work. Nature invented all of these millions of years ago. That is what joints are. Even some of the early animals without backbones had ingenious joints, and just think of a spider's legs!

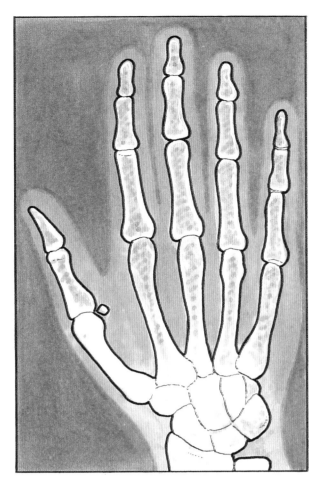

An X-ray shows the many joints in a human hand.

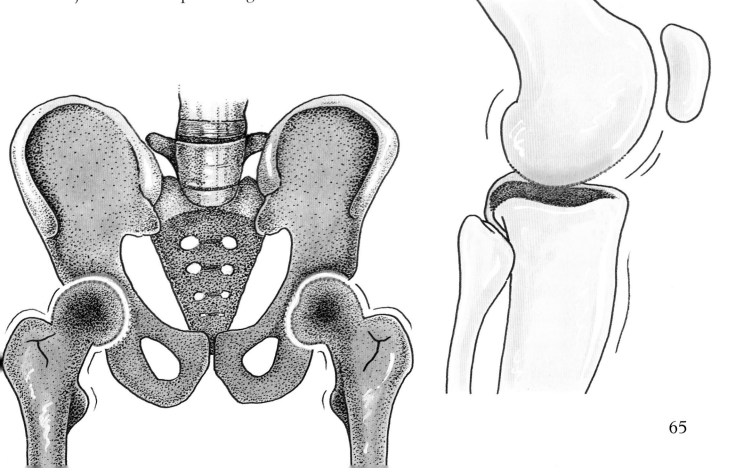

Nervous?

Do you know which cells in your body make your muscles work? The answer is your nerve cells, but they do much, much, more than that. Nerve cells send electrical signals around your body – signals that make you see, hear, smell, taste, feel, touch, think, learn and remember, as well as move. They are some of the most interesting cells in your body – and they come in amazing shapes and sizes.

It is easy to understand how nerve cells can control your body if you first understand how a single nerve cell works. The job of every nerve cell is to collect and send information very quickly around your body, like a microscopic wire in a complicated electrical machine. One end of the nerve cell has many fine branches called dendrites (*den-drites*). Dendrites receive information. This information is turned into an electric signal that speeds along a very long thin strand of its cytoplasm called an axon. Axons are very thin, less than one millionth of a yard wide, but they can be very long – some axons that travel to and from the muscles in your legs are over one yard long! Finally, the axon divides into a number of microscopic branches each ending in a little flat disc. The discs transmit signals to the nearest nerve cell, or to other cells whose action it controls – muscle cells for instance.

Nerve cells receive information about changes in temperature, vibrations, light, pressure or chemicals. They are found in your eyes, ears, mouth, nose, skin, muscles, joints and in many places inside your body. Other nerve cells carry this information as electrical signals to more nerve cells, or to muscle cells.

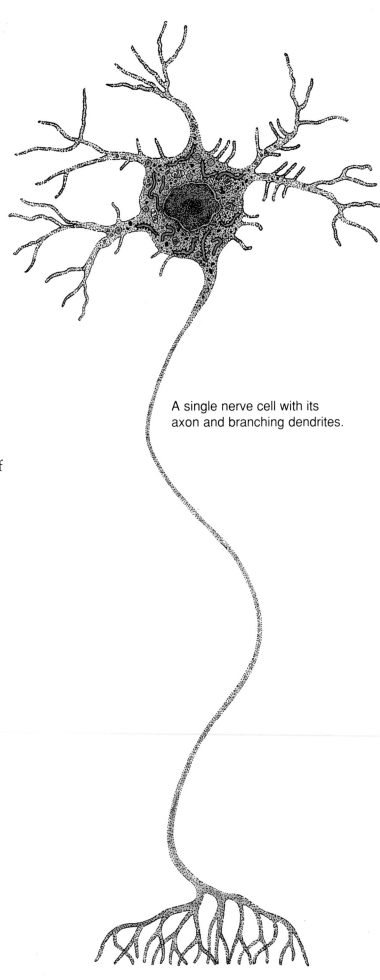

A single nerve cell with its axon and branching dendrites.

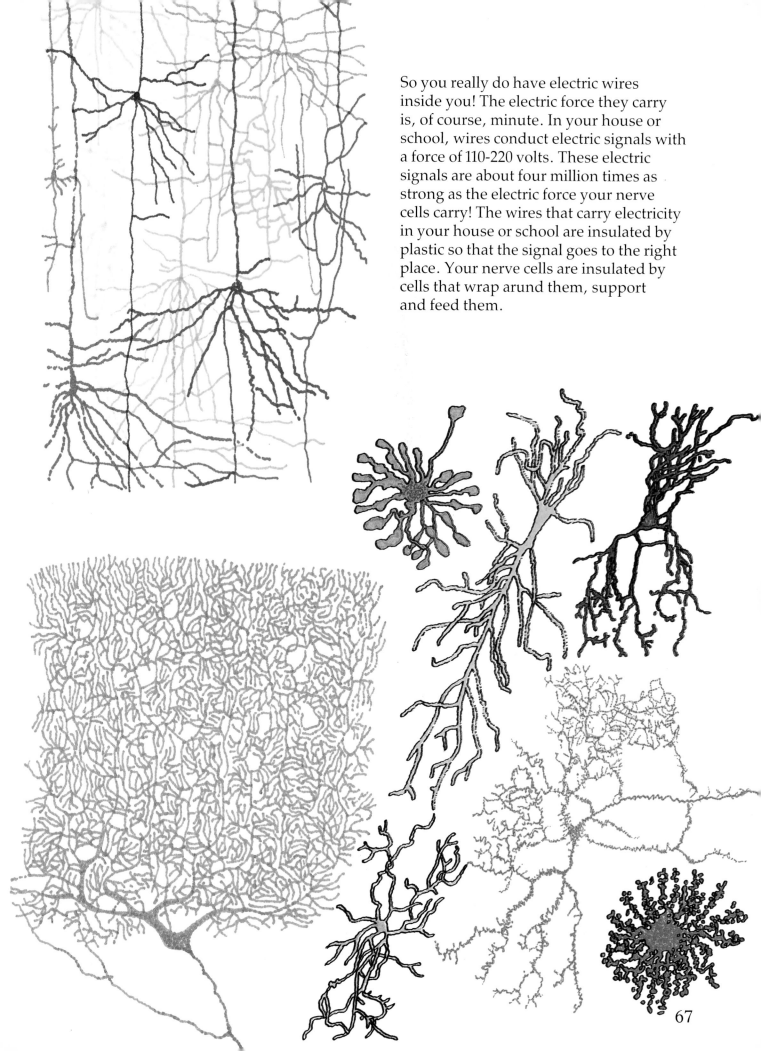

So you really do have electric wires inside you! The electric force they carry is, of course, minute. In your house or school, wires conduct electric signals with a force of 110-220 volts. These electric signals are about four million times as strong as the electric force your nerve cells carry! The wires that carry electricity in your house or school are insulated by plastic so that the signal goes to the right place. Your nerve cells are insulated by cells that wrap arund them, support and feed them.

67

Nerve cells work together in a network called the nervous system that spreads all over your body. Each nerve is a bundle of millions of nerve cell axons plus cells that protect them and blood vessels. Nerves carry messages to and from your brain and spinal cord. Thirty-one pairs of nerves leave the spinal cord. Very soon they split into branches which split into smaller branches, and so on, until all parts of your body are reached by nerves. All information from your body concerning touch, pain, temperature, pressure, vibration and sense of position comes from these nerves. Another 12 pairs of nerves come straight from the brain and go to the eyes, ears, mouth and nose, and to muscles in the head and neck. They also serve the digestive system, heart, blood vessels and lungs. These parts of your nervous system are under automatic control. You don't have to tell your heart to beat, or the muscles of your small intestine to pump food around, do you?

Nerves carry electrical messages around your body but they don't analyze them and make new signals. This happens in your brain.

Your brain is like a collection of hundreds of computers working together so that you see, hear, smell, touch and respond to the world outside you, and think, learn and remember. Different parts of your brain do quite different jobs. For instance, your hypothalamus (*high-po-thal-am-us*) maintains a constant environment inside you, and your cerebellum (*ser-ee-bell-um*) coordinates your muscles and balance.

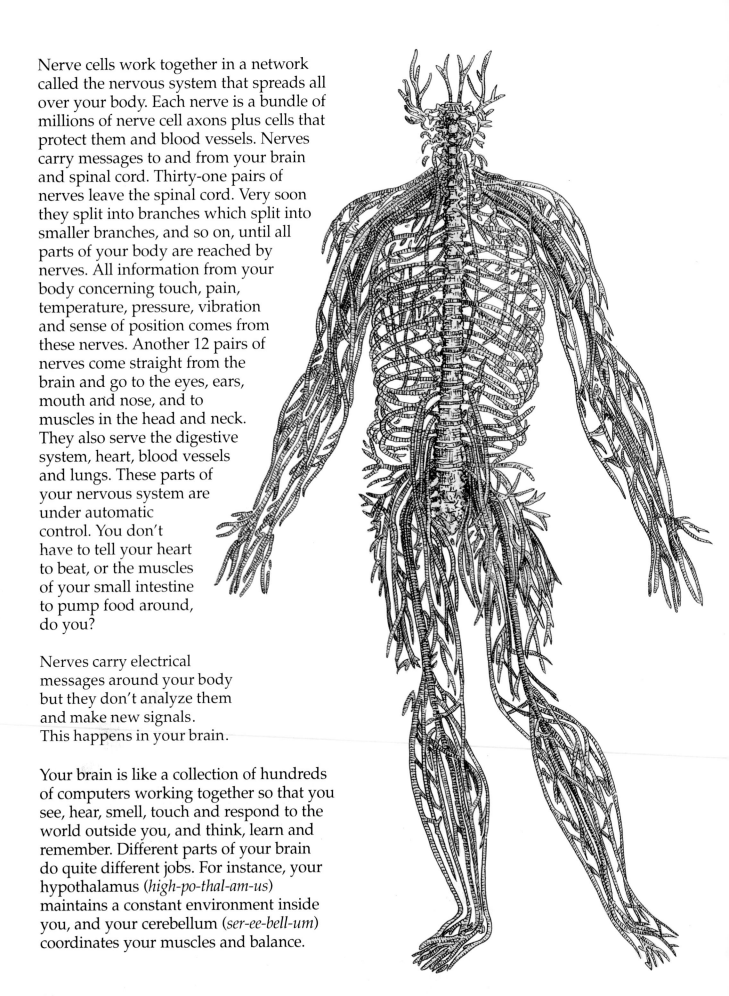

Scientists are only beginning to understand how all of these actions are controlled by an ever-changing network of millions of nerve cells that connect in millions of ways with millions more nerve cells.

The part of the brain that makes us humans different from all other animals is the cerebral cortex (*ser-ee-brall cor-tex*). This is much larger in humans, relative to body size, than in any other animal. It handles messages from your five senses (sight, sound, touch, taste and smell); controls highly skilled and complicated muscle movements; and enables you to paint pictures, play musical instruments, understand speech and language, write stories and solve puzzles. Also, and maybe most importantly, your ability to think and remember is there in the cerebral cortex.

1. Vision

2. Hearing

3. Understanding speech and sound

4. Movement

5. Taste

6. Touch

7. Balance and muscle coordination

8. Cerebral cortex (see text)

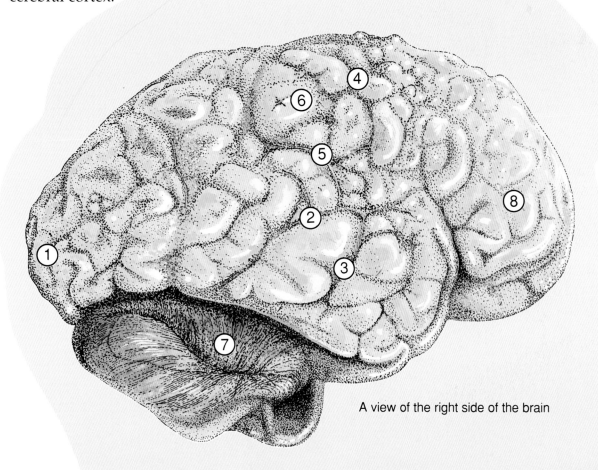

A view of the right side of the brain

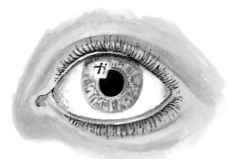

If your brain is like the most complicated network of computers ever known, your eyes are like very advanced cameras, (even if they don't produce photographs!). Your eyes are protected by your eyebrows (they stop sweat dropping in), eyelids and a thin film of tears. They have two lenses that focus rays of light into a tiny upside down and back to front image on the inside surface of the eyeball, called the retina.

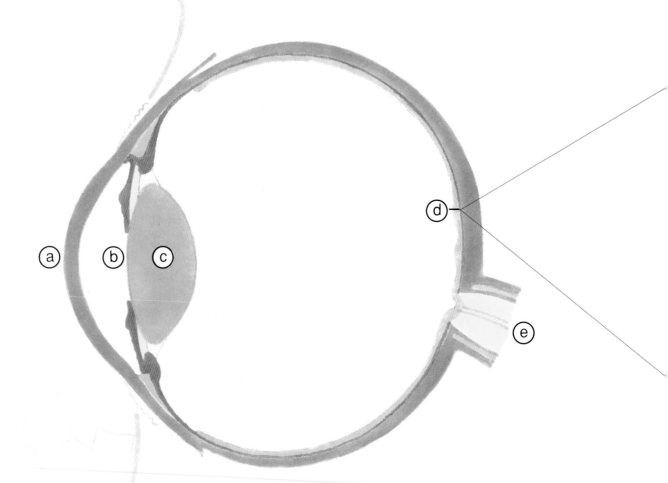

a. Cornea (which is the first lens)

b. Iris (the colored part of your eye)

c. Lens

d. Retina

e. The optic nerve leaves from here

The retina is only about two-hundredths of an inch thick, but it is the most remarkable tissue of the eye, if not your whole body. The retina receives light signals, converts them to electrical nerve signals, processes a lot of the information, and then sends this information along the optic nerve to the brain.

This is a drawing of the cells of the retina magnified about four hundred times. Light has to pass right through the retina before it meets the cells that respond to it, the rods and cones. There are about one hundred million rod cells and seven million cone cells. Rod cells respond in dim light, cone cells respond to color and detail. Behind these cells, at the very back of the retina, is a layer of cells full of melanin pigment that absorb stray light and stop it reflecting back.

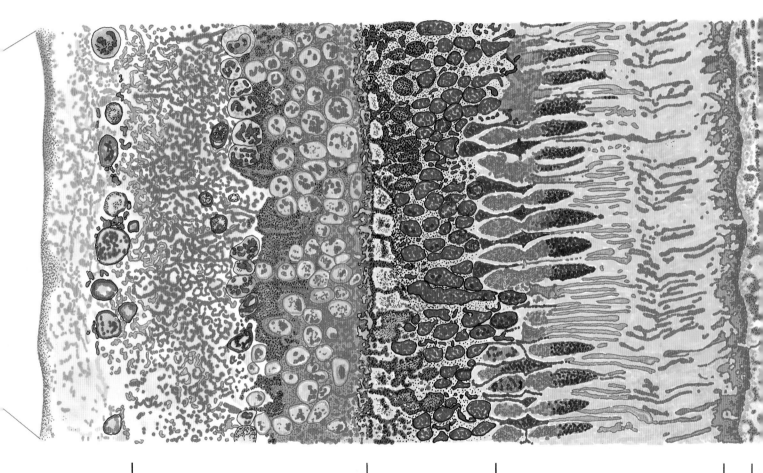

| Nerve fiber layer | Outer nerve cell layer | Inner nerve cell layer | Rods and cones |

Pigment cells

When rods and cones are hit by a ray of light, they send an electrical signal, back the way the light wave came, to a layer of nerve cells. These cells transmit and process information through their axons and dendrites to the next layer. About one million nerve cells join together in the optic nerve, which carries this information, upside down and back to front, to the brain. It is your brain that really sees, when it has decoded all the information about shape, color and pattern that the rods and cones received.

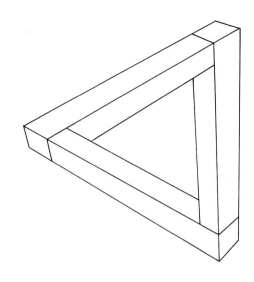

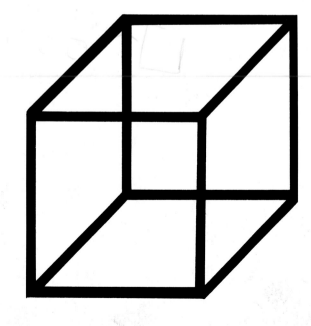

Can water really run uphill?
The answer, according to the famous
Dutch artist Escher seems to be yes!

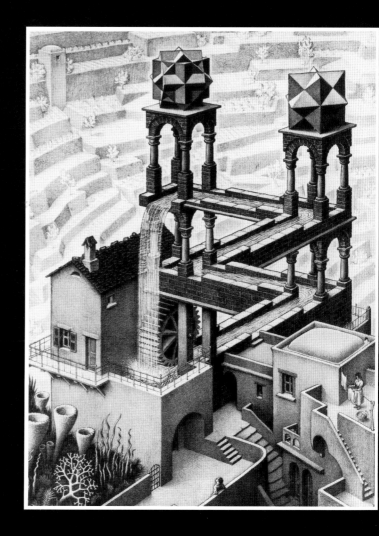

Your brain cells find some of these
pictures impossible because they
know that no object can be in two
places at the same time or be more
than one size or shape. In the other
pictures, your brain cells keep on
changing your mind about the
picture you "see"!

Now, what about your ears? You may think they stick out too far, but those floppy bits are one important part of your very sophisticated sound system. Think of what most people can hear. Gentle sounds, like a breeze rustling leaves on a summer's day; intricate sounds, like bird song at dawn; or loud sounds like a rock band or a supersonic jet.

How does your sound system work? Well, as you might have guessed, nerve cells and your brain are involved. The parts of your ears that you can see channel sound waves from all around down a narrow tube lined with cells that produce sticky wax. The wax stops the skin from drying out and protects the inner ear form dust and dirt. Sound waves then hit your eardrum. This makes three tiny bones in your middle ear vibrate. This vibration is recorded in your inner ear, one inch inside your head. The inner ear is made of many canals and cavities that spiral like a helter-skelter. They are filled with fluid. Touching this fluid are some very special cells with tiny hairs on their surface. The vibrating bones change the pressure of the fluid and move these tiny hairs. This sends an electrical signal to nerve cells attached to them. These signals are collected into a nerve that goes to the brain.

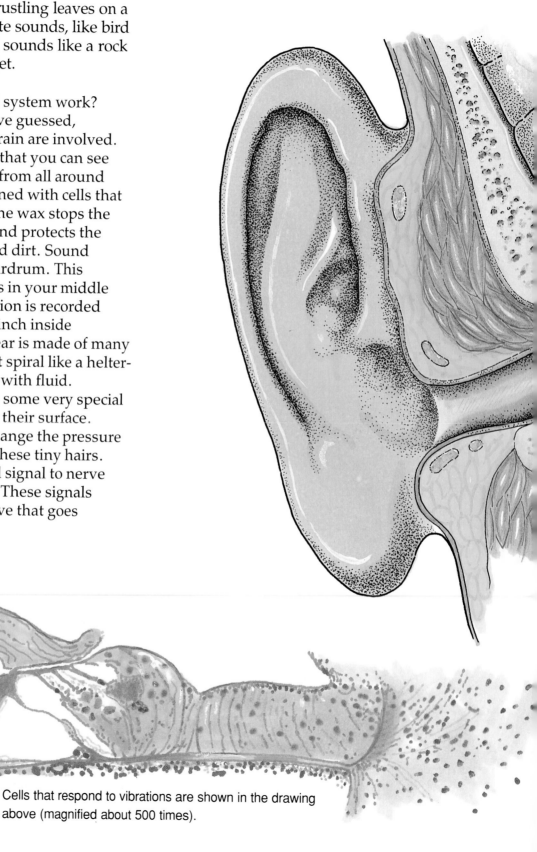

Cells that respond to vibrations are shown in the drawing above (magnified about 500 times).

74

But your ears don't just allow you to hear: without some parts of your inner ear you would be very dizzy! That's because three loopy canals in your inner ear control your sense of balance. Jelly-like fluid in these canals moves as your head twists and turns and makes hairy cells send signals to your brain.

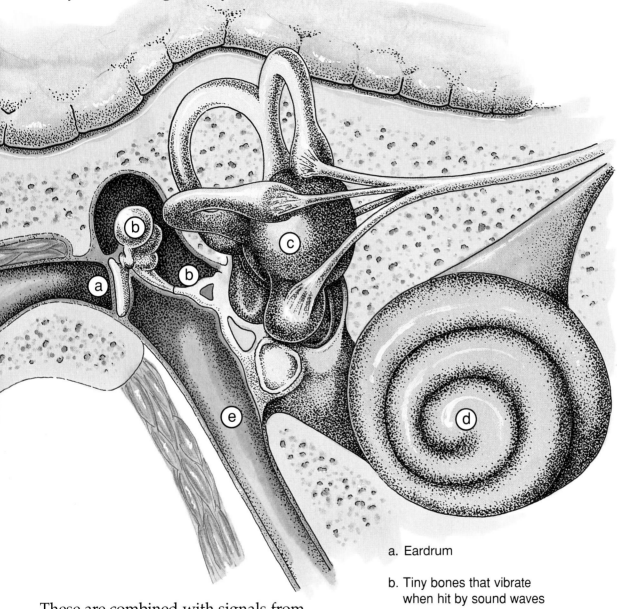

These are combined with signals from your eyes that tell your brain where your body is in relation to its surroundings. Without all these electrical messages you would find it very difficult to walk in a straight line. You would be unable to stand upright on a moving staircase or ship, or to run up a spiral staircase, let alone walk a tightrope!

a. Eardrum

b. Tiny bones that vibrate when hit by sound waves

c. The parts of your ear that keep you well-balanced

d. The canals and cavities that are filled with fluid and cells that respond to vibrations

e. This tube goes to the back of your tonsils. It makes the pressure equal on each side of your eardrum.

How do you smell? Well at the top of your nose cavity, just under your brain, is an area of cells, about three-quarters of an inch wide, that contains your olfactory (*oll-factory*) cells. Normally the air that you breathe does not reach this high up, but when you sniff, the air is channelled over this very moist area. But what exactly do you smell? The only substances that you can smell are gases released from complex chemicals. The more gases they release, the smellier they are – like the chemicals in rotten fish, petrol, perfume, or in very ripe cheese. The gases you sniff up your nose dissolve in the liquid mucus that covers the olfactory cells. Olfactory cells are hairy cells rather like the cells in your ears that allow you to hear and keep your balance. But up your nose, they send electrical signals to your brain when triggered by smelly gases dissolved in the mucus.

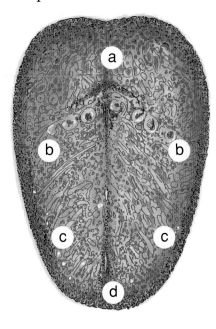

You may think that your sense of smell just helps you know when your dog needs a bath or when your favorite meal is cooking in the oven, but it is much more important than that. Electrical signals from olfactory cells are carried all the way to a very important part of your brain that controls your moods, memories and emotions. Think about smells that once made you happy, sad or frightened. Smell them again and the memories come flooding back. Oh no, not your socks!

Your sense of smell is much stronger than your sense of taste, and the smell of your food tells your brain a lot more than its taste. Think about times when you have a bad cold. You cannot smell and the food you eat is almost tasteless. Other nerve cells in your tongue send information to your brain about the texture of your food, and if you eat very spicy food with lots of chilli pepper or mustard in it, pain receptors in your tongue send some very strong messages to your brain – glass of water quick!

yuck!

a. Bitter

b. Sour

c. Salty

d. Sweet

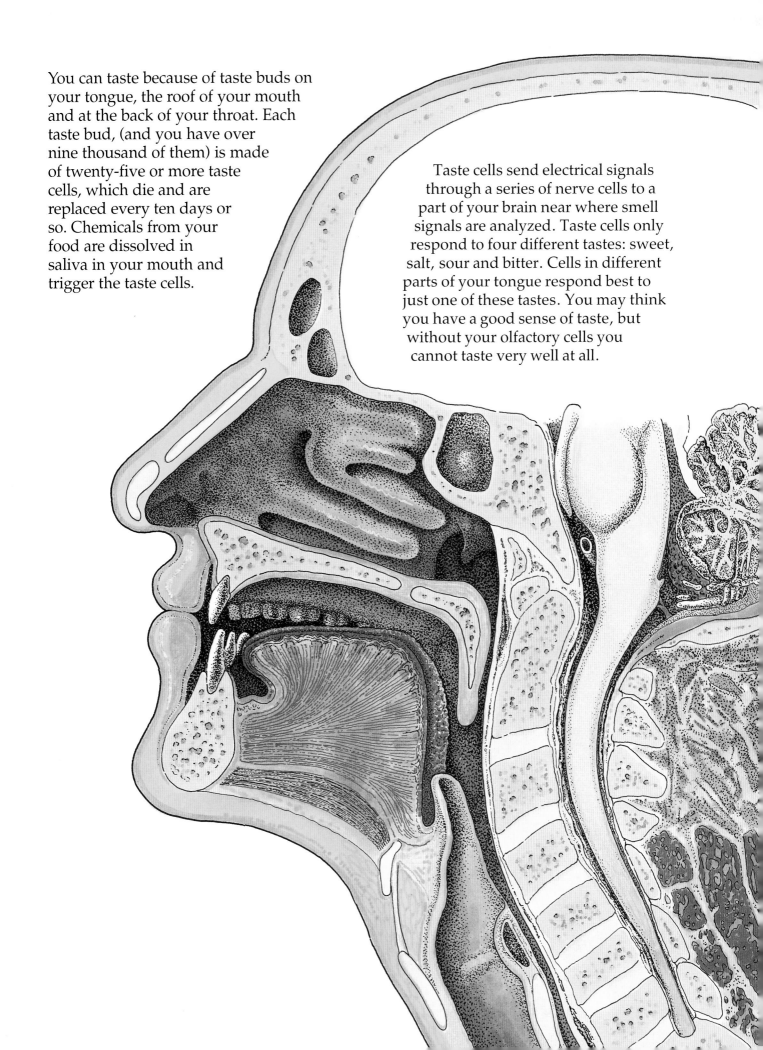

You can taste because of taste buds on your tongue, the roof of your mouth and at the back of your throat. Each taste bud, (and you have over nine thousand of them) is made of twenty-five or more taste cells, which die and are replaced every ten days or so. Chemicals from your food are dissolved in saliva in your mouth and trigger the taste cells.

Taste cells send electrical signals through a series of nerve cells to a part of your brain near where smell signals are analyzed. Taste cells only respond to four different tastes: sweet, salt, sour and bitter. Cells in different parts of your tongue respond best to just one of these tastes. You may think you have a good sense of taste, but without your olfactory cells you cannot taste very well at all.

Everything Under Control?

Your body is under constant attack from deadly invisible enemies intent on making you ill! But don't worry. Many of the cells that make up the human body have ingenious ways of protecting you from beastly germs.

Some cells make barriers to stop enemies getting inside your body. Very few germs can penetrate that thick tough layer of dead skin cells that covers the surface of your body. If you breathe in germs, they get stuck in a gloppy protein called mucus (*mew-cuss*). Then tiny hairs in the tubes of your nose and lungs waft them outside again. If you swallow dangerous germs, the acid in your stomach usually kills them, if they haven't already been destroyed by the germ-killing chemicals in saliva. Even your tears will kill germs!

But sometimes invisible germs break through all these defenses and get right into your body. If they aren't stopped they could take over your body and destroy it! But don't let it bother you. You are the owner of a daring and highly organized band of cells always on full alert from the enemy attack.

We're going to introduce you to three of the most important types of these cells:
neutrophils (*new-tro-fils*)
macrophages (*mac-ro-fay-jes*)
and lymphocytes (*lim-fo-sites*).

Otherwise known as…

78

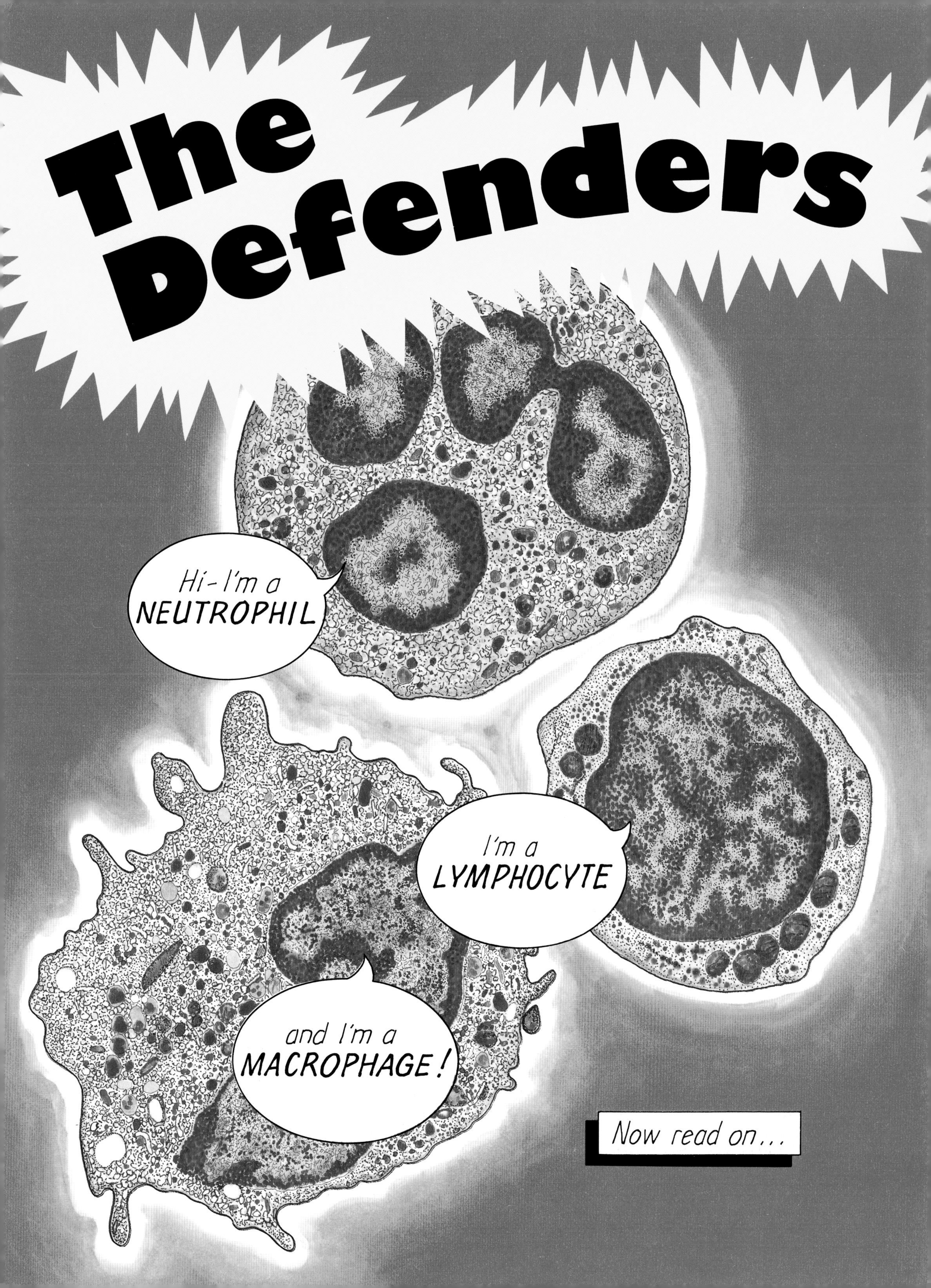
The Defenders
Hi-I'm a NEUTROPHIL
I'm a LYMPHOCYTE
and I'm a MACROPHAGE!
Now read on...

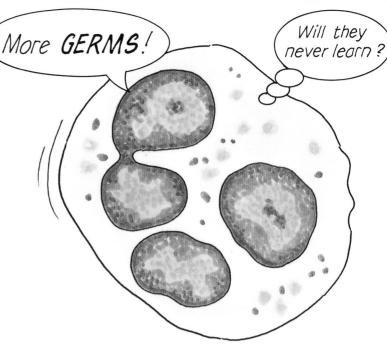

Neutrophils are one important fighting force in your defender cell army. They constantly patrol the blood armed with powerful chemicals that can exterminate germs in an instant. When neutrophils detect invading germs, they squeeze through the nearest blood vessel into the trouble zone.

They gobble up the germ and then destroy it with deadly chemical weapons they have stored inside them. The germ soon dies – unfortunately, so does the neutrophil. Don't worry. There are plenty more neutrophils where they came from.

(Did you know that pus is made of millions and millions of dead neutrophils?).

Every minute of every day cells in your bone marrow make eighty million neutrophils to replace those that die of wear and tear and fighting bugs!

Neutrophils find a spot of trouble.

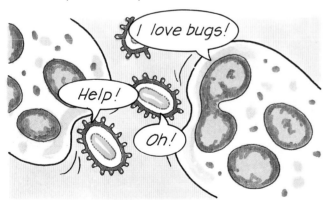

They gobble up the tasty germs …

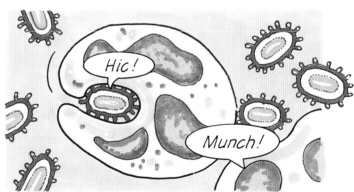

… and destroy them with chemical weapons.

The germs soon die – but so do the neutrophils

Macrophages are the waste disposal experts of your defender cell army. They clear up the mess whenever you are ill or injured, and wherever germs and dirt collect. Macrophages also patrol the blood, and they lurk in many parts of your body where germs might attack.

There are millions of macrophages in your lungs, for instance, continually eating up the dust and germs that you breathe in every day. Like neutrophils, they are full of germ-zapping chemicals, but they live a lot longer. Macrophages don't usually self destruct when they zap germs. This is because they have another vital role to play in the army.

Before they completely destroy germs they have captured, they show them to the third force in the defender cell army, the lymphocytes. This warns the lymphocytes that there's trouble afoot and they join the battle.

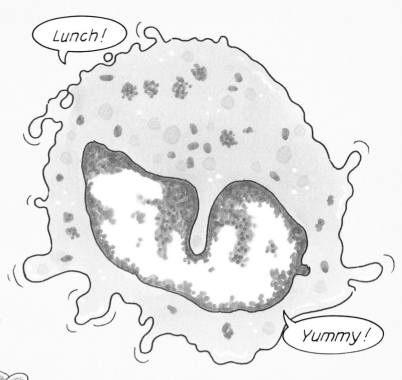

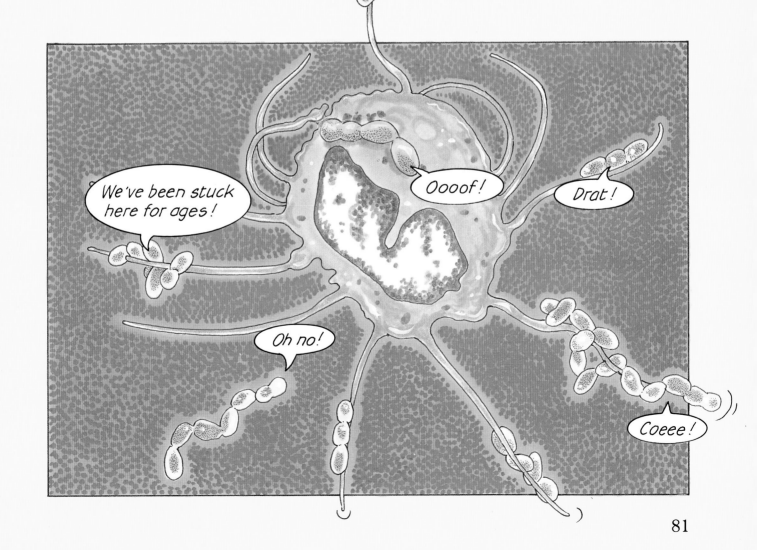

Lymphocytes are the cleverest members of your defender cell army. There are about one million million of them in your body. Your bone marrow makes one thousand million new ones every day to replace those that die.

The lymphocyte force is organized into thousands and thousands of squads. Different lymphocyte squads are programmed to attack different germs.

You may not believe it, but for every germ that you are likely to meet there is a lymphocyte squad in your body all ready to attack. When a lymphocyte squad meets its enemy, the cells multiply into a large force all ready to fight just that particular germ.

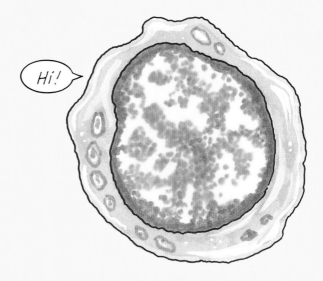

Lymphocytes make special weapons called antibodies that stick tightly to the germ. Antibodies stop the germ working and make it especially tasty for macrophages and neutrophils to gobble up.

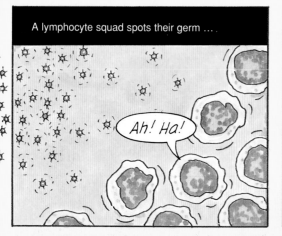

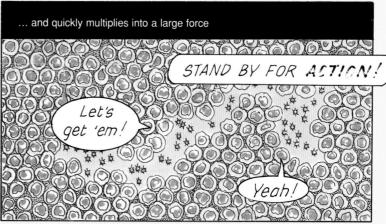

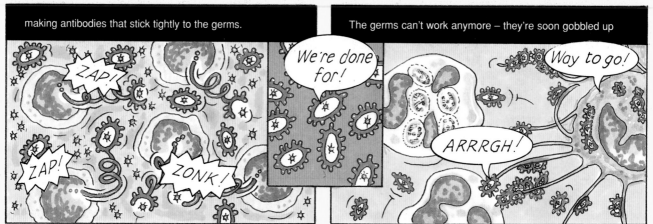

Other members of the squad become killer cells that destroy germ-infected cells before they can do any harm. Killer cells punch holes in cell membranes. Once a cell has been punctured, all its important chemicals begin to leak out and it shrivels and dies. Hopefully the germs die with it! When the battle is won, the squad is larger than before. Some lymphocytes remain on alert for their particular germ for many years.

If that germ dares to invade again, the squad will attack in double-quick time! Lymphocytes, macrophages and neutrophils send each other messages using special chemicals called cytokines (*sight-toe-kines*). Cytokines summon cells to a trouble spot, turn peaceful lymphocytes into killer cells, and make macrophages and neutrophils absolutely ravenous for germs.

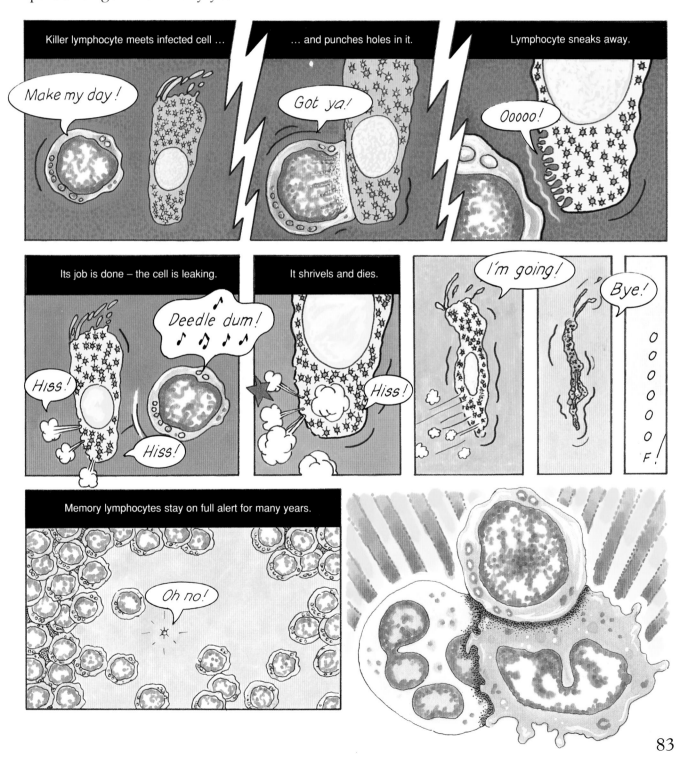

83

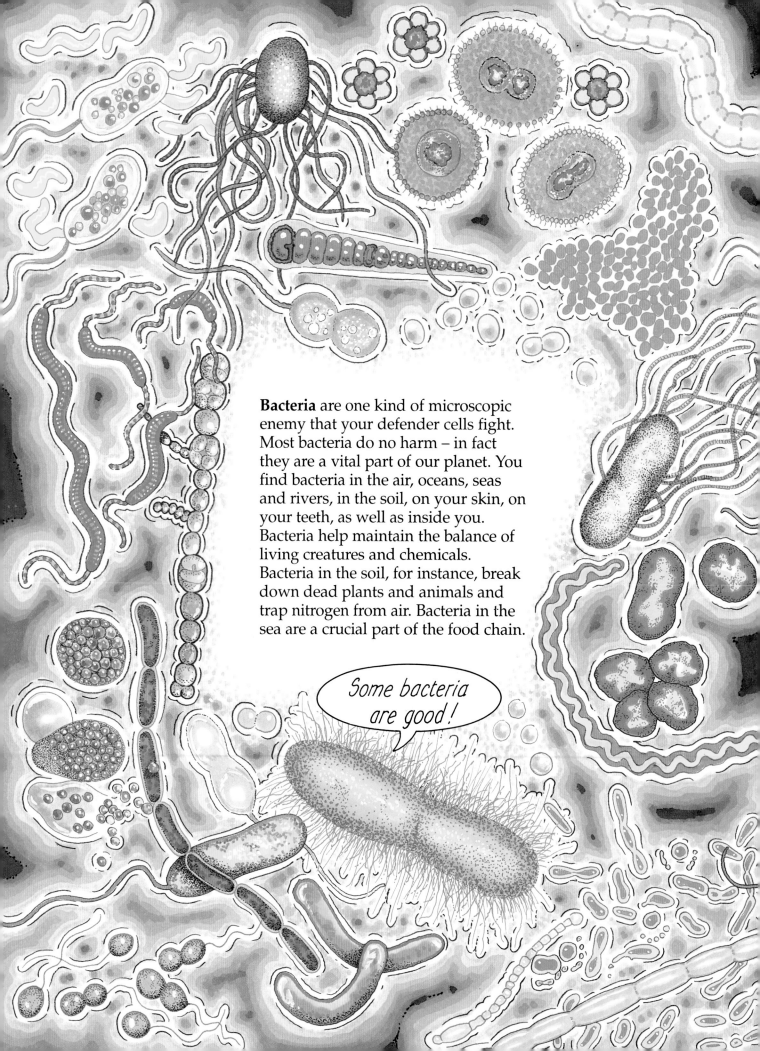

Bacteria are one kind of microscopic enemy that your defender cells fight. Most bacteria do no harm – in fact they are a vital part of our planet. You find bacteria in the air, oceans, seas and rivers, in the soil, on your skin, on your teeth, as well as inside you. Bacteria help maintain the balance of living creatures and chemicals. Bacteria in the soil, for instance, break down dead plants and animals and trap nitrogen from air. Bacteria in the sea are a crucial part of the food chain.

Some bacteria are good!

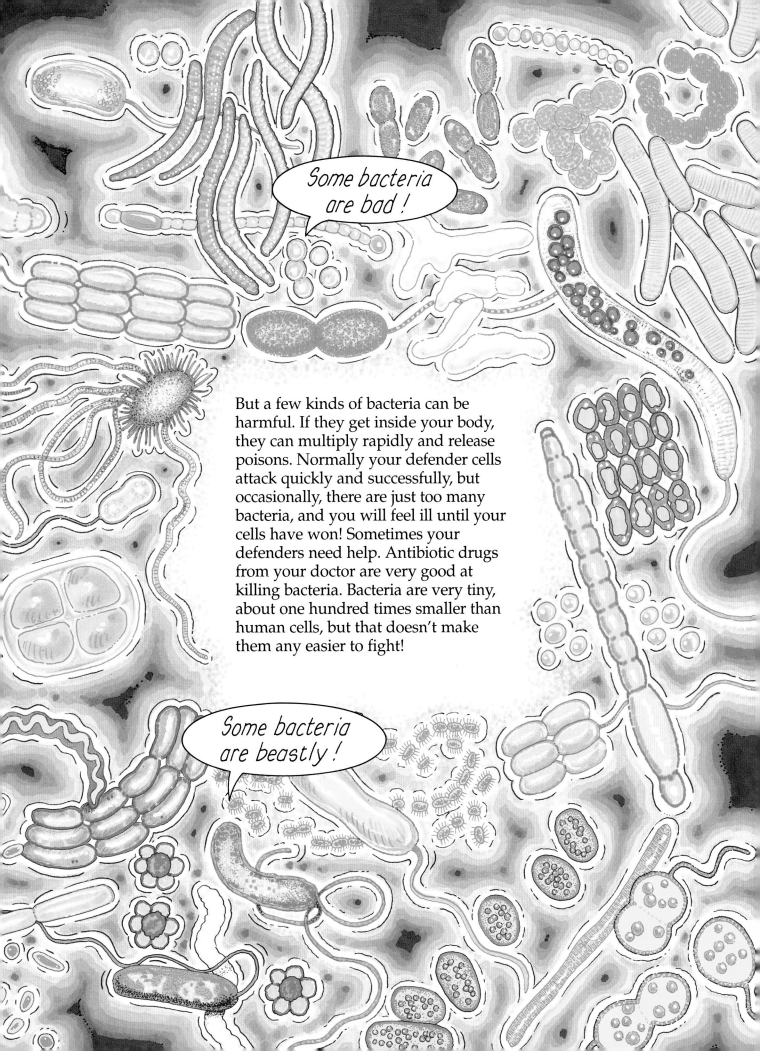

Some bacteria are bad!

But a few kinds of bacteria can be harmful. If they get inside your body, they can multiply rapidly and release poisons. Normally your defender cells attack quickly and successfully, but occasionally, there are just too many bacteria, and you will feel ill until your cells have won! Sometimes your defenders need help. Antibiotic drugs from your doctor are very good at killing bacteria. Bacteria are very tiny, about one hundred times smaller than human cells, but that doesn't make them any easier to fight!

Some bacteria are beastly!

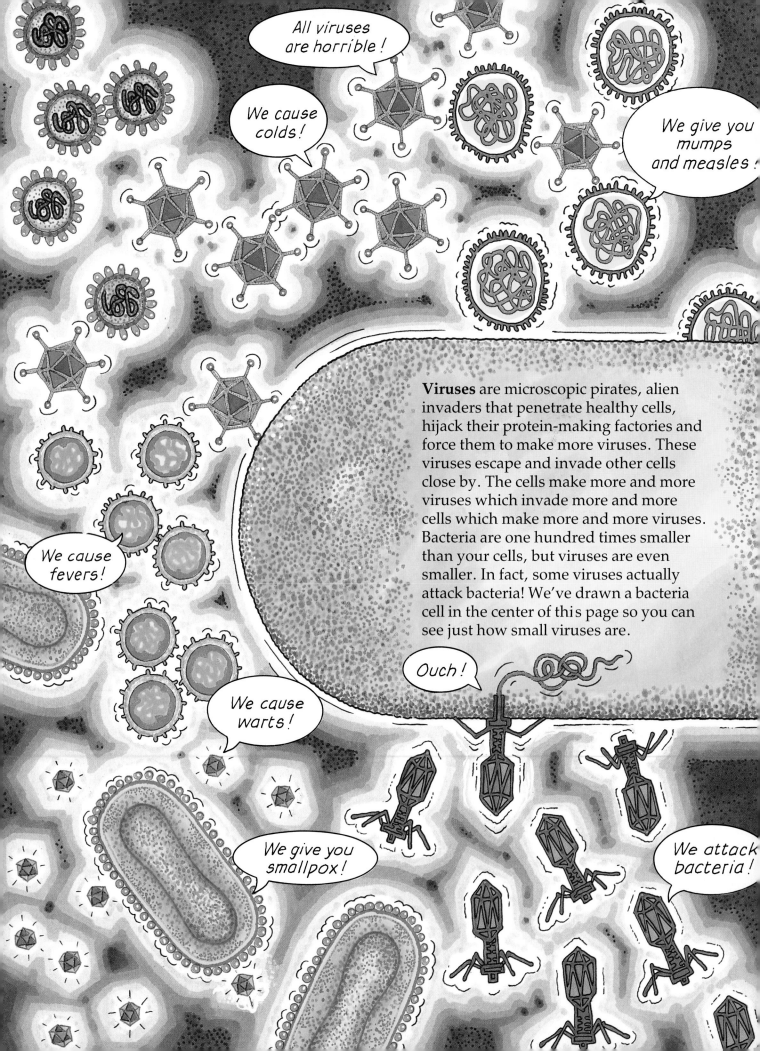

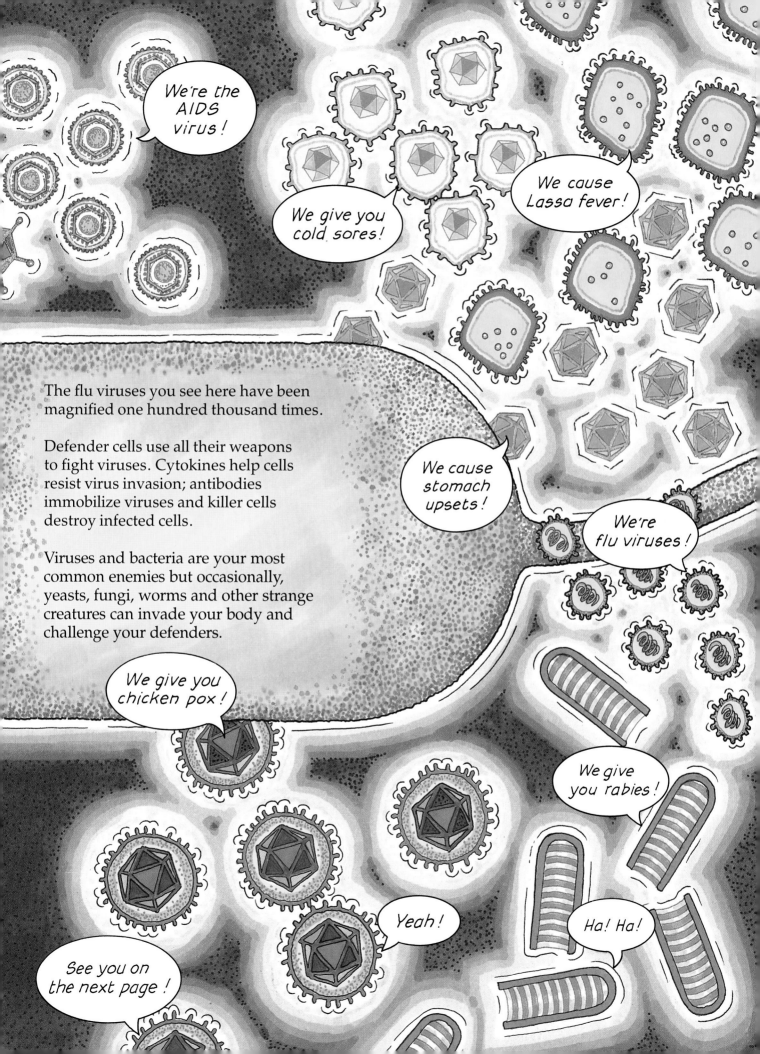

1. Well about two weeks ago you must have breathed in a few million of his chicken pox viruses.

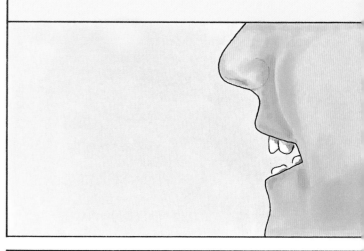

2. The viruses invaded some of the cells up your nose and began to multiply and spread to cells close by. Your defender cells quickly spotted them!

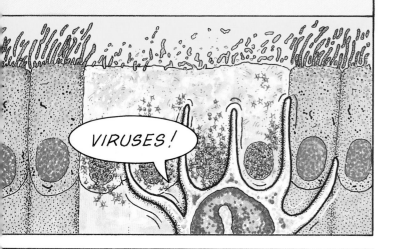

3. Your macrophages alerted lymphocytes in the nearest lymph node. Lymphocyte squads programmed to fight chicken pox began to expand and make antibodies.

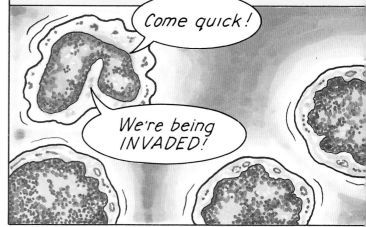

4. Those antibodies were not able to stop the virus spreading to your lymph nodes and all round your body, but you still felt O.K.

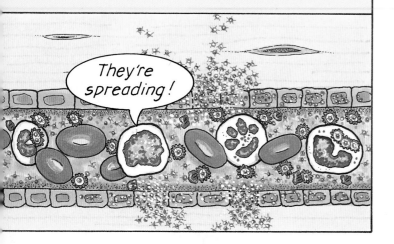

5. After about two weeks there were millions and millions of viruses zooming round your blood and lymphatic system, trying to get to their favorite target, skin cells. Now you began to feel ill!

88

6. The viruses began to grow in your skin, which became red and itchy.

7. Dying skin cells began to swell up and fluid began to leak out, followed by millions of neutrophils. That is why you are   very spotty!

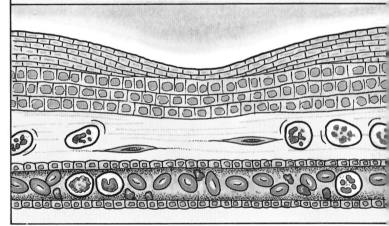

8. DON'T PANIC!! Your defenders have not given up. They have been making their most powerful antibodies as well as cytokines to protect cells from virus invasion, and most importantly, killer cells.

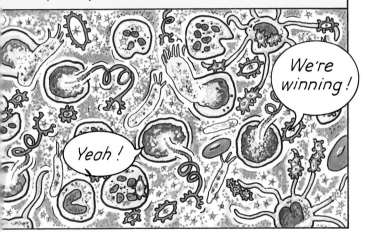

9. The defenders will win (they always do except in very rare cases) and clear up the mess! Builder cells called fibroblasts (*fye-bro-blasts*) will repair the skin as new skin cells begin to grow over each spot.

10. The good news is that anti-chicken pox lymphocyte squads will remain on full alert for a very long time. You will not get chicken pox again! But have they destroyed all the viruses ...?

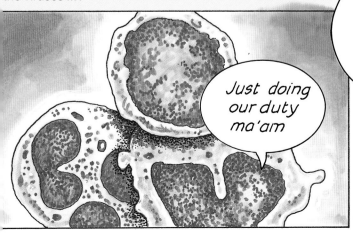

1. Your defender cells also do important work in a wound. Cut skin bleeds because tiny blood vessels are sliced open. Platelets in the blood stick to the damaged vessel. Chemicals released by platelets make the blood vessel contract and summon extra platelets to plug the hole. Blood that has leaked into the wound turns into a gell full of fibers which help make the clot.

2. Neutrophils nearby sense the danger and crawl through blood vessels into the wound. Macrophages are close behind. They have to clear up all the dead cells, bacteria and general rubbish in the wound. They also send out chemical messages that get other cells working and keep them under control.

1. Have you ever broken one of your bones? A broken bone bleeds just like skin and a blood clot soon forms. Neutrophils and macrophages move in and new blood vessels begin to grow into the gap. Medical help is usually needed to hold the bone in its proper position with a cast or a splint while it begins to heal.

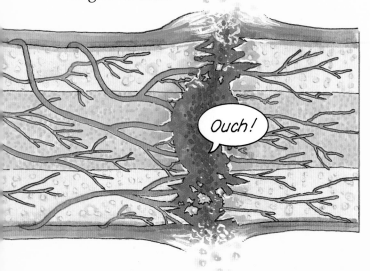

2. Fibroblasts begin to make collagen ropes that join the broken ends of the bone together. Bone-making osteoblasts and cartilage-making chondrocytes (*con-dro-sites*) soon start their work, laying down cartilage and fragile bone in a rather lumpy way.

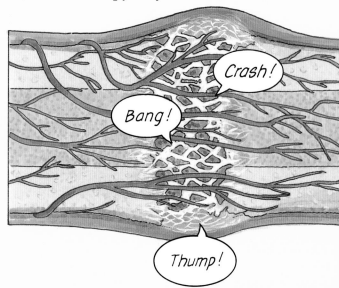

3. Just a few hours after the trouble began, cells from the top layer of skin begin to crawl across the gap using a shaky scaffolding of fibers from clotted blood. Beneath them, builder fibroblasts start moving in and multiplying, Fibroblasts begin to make lots of collagen protein that assembles into microscopic ropes to pull the sides of the cut together.

4. New skin cells multiply to make a thick outside layer. The scab will soon fall off. Underneath, the fibroblasts are still repairing and strengthening the wound. The tiny blood vessels have been repaired as well. Sometimes a cut can be very large and deep, and cells have trouble holding the edges together. Then doctors and nurses help out by stitching the edges of the wound together.

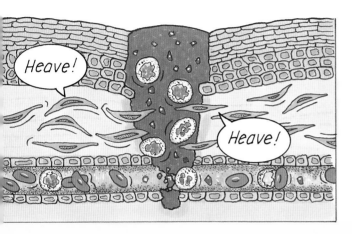

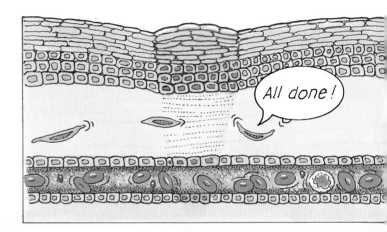

3. More osteoblasts move in from healthy bone nearby and begin to make a stronger repair that joins together fragments of dead and living bone.

4. In come the osteoclasts. They act as sculptors, modelling the bone back to its original shape. The bone becomes stronger and stronger and can soon do its usual job again. Children's cells are particularly good at mending bone; they do it twice as fast as grown-ups!

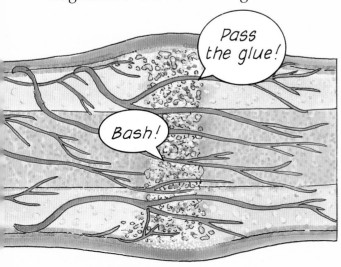

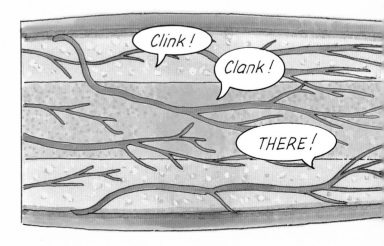

1. We have told you in this book how well behaved your cells are and how they always work together to keep you fit, healthy and growing in the right way. If a cell starts to misbehave and go out of control, it can make someone ill. That is called **cancer**.

2. A cancer cell starts behaving differently from the cells around it because its DNA plans have been damaged. The cell stops doing its proper job, starts to multiply uncontrollably and pushes the normal cells out of the way.

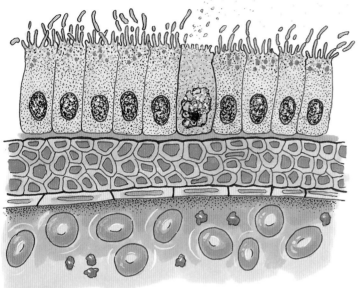

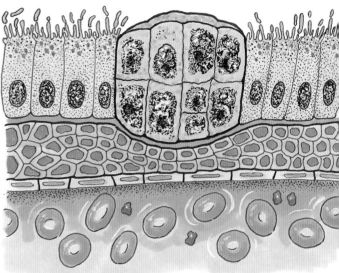

3. Worse still, some cancer cells can break out into the bloodstream and invade other places in the body. It is very unusual for a child to get cancer. Cancer is more common in very old people, because most cancer cells take a long time to get really out of control.

4. The good news is that nowadays doctors and scientists understand a lot more about cancer and how to make people better. Over half the people who get cancer can be cured, by skillful surgery or powerful drugs and by special rays that destroy cancer cells.

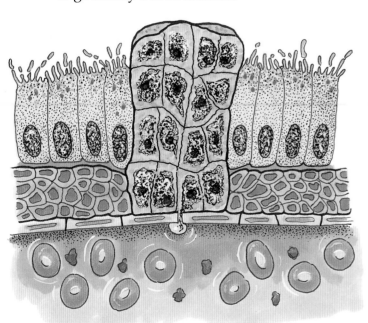

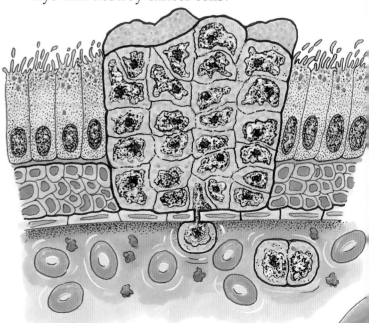

92

Scientists don't know why some children get cancer, but you can reduce your chances of getting cancer when you are older. First of all, don't start smoking. Cigarette smoke is full of cancer-causing chemicals and it damages your heart as well (apart from making you smell like an old ashtray!). Second, don't spend too long in the sun unless your skin is covered with clothing or sun-block cream, especially if you have a pale complexion. Third, eat plenty of fresh citrus fruit and green leafy vegetables.

One of the ways that the cells of your body are controlled to work together is by chemical messages called **hormones**. Hormones are usually made by cells in one part of the body and travel in the blood to deliver their message to different cells in another part of the body. Your body can make at least twenty different hormones. Hormones help control the way your cells use up food substances and release energy; and they help control the level of sugar, salt and water in your body. Hormones generally act on cells quite slowly and over long periods of time, but two hormones that act quickly are called adrenaline (*ad-ren-al-in*) and noradrenaline. They are produced by the adrenal (*ad-rean-all*) glands that sit above your kidneys. You may already have experienced what these two hormones do to your cells. Have you ever been *really* frightened? Just imagine that this happened to you …

…you decide to raid the fridge for a midnight snack. As you tiptoe down the stairs, an owl hoots eerily in the swaying trees outside. Your heart begins to beat harder and faster. You hear a rustling, scuffling noise in the kitchen. Your breathing is rapid and your skin feels cold and clammy. With pounding heart, you move cautiously along the hallway.

Silence…Suddenly you see a ghostly face in the hallway mirror! But it's your own reflection, pale skin, eyes wide open with dilated pupils! From the kitchen comes a strange sound, a muffled guzzling and hissing noise. Your face and hands are sweating, you feel the hair rising on the back of your neck. Slowly you push open the kitchen door. You see nothing unusual. By now your mouth feels so dry, you must have a drink. An ice-cold glass of milk will calm your nerves. But as you reach for the fridge, the door starts to open…

All these changes to your body happened because your brain sent urgent danger signals to your adrenal glands. The hormones they released sent messages to muscle, skin, nerve and blood vessel cells. Billions of cells all over your body changed their jobs so that you could run away extremely quickly or stand and fight. Doctors call adrenaline and noradrenaline the "fight or flight" hormones – you can see why!

CREEEEK!

Chance in a Billion

When children reach that "certain age," things start to alter, inside and outside their bodies – all because of hormones called **sex hormones**. In girls, most of the hormones are produced in ovaries (*oav-a-rees*), two small almond-shaped parts that are found close to the uterus (*you-ter-us*) (womb). Ovaries are full of eggs that can make new human beings. As a girl begins to grow up, hormones produced by the ovaries make the egg cells mature. About once a month, one egg is released from one of the ovaries and is captured by a tiny tube that joins to the uterus, called the fallopian (*fal-oh-pee-an*) tube. Once the ovaries begin to release eggs, the girl will start having periods or menstruation (*men-strew-a-shon*). The hormones also instruct cells around the nipples to start dividing at a very fast rate and breasts develop. Hormones deliver messages to skin cells in the pubic and underarm regions so that hair starts growing, and to bone and joint cells so that the hips begin to widen.

The hormone that turns boys into men is produced by their testes (the sperm-making parts). The hormone instructs skin cells, especially of the face, to make a lot more hair. This hair is much stronger than the fine hair that covers a child's body. Boys start growing beards (unless they shave). Their voices deepen because of changes in the cells of the voice box (larynx). Hormones change a boy's skeleton so that his shoulders grow broader, and hormones instruct the cells of the testes to make sperm. Sperm are tiny cells with long tails, which look a bit like tadpoles.

If sperm are made in the man's testes and eggs in the woman's ovaries, how do they meet? You may already know that when a man and a woman make love, they can be making life as well! The man's penis becomes firm and enters the woman's vagina (*vaj-ine-a*). Sperm are stored in the epididymis (*ep-ee-did-ee-mis*), which surrounds the testes. When they are released, they travel at high speed through the penis. The sperm, mixed with sugar-containing fluid to give them energy, are discharged into the vagina by powerful contractions of the man's pelvic muscles.

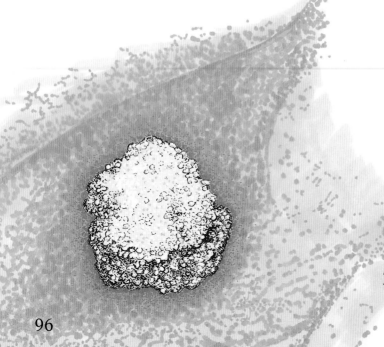

An egg in a fallopian tube surrounded by thousands of cells making food for it.

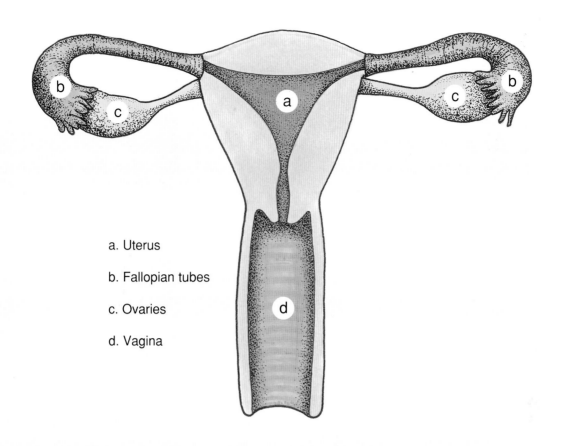

a. Uterus

b. Fallopian tubes

c. Ovaries

d. Vagina

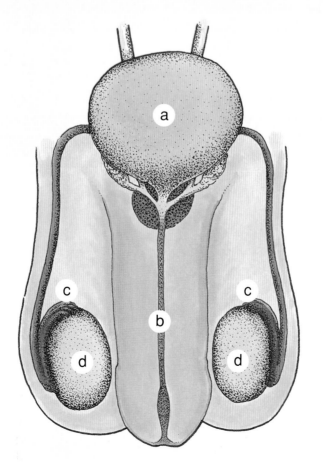

a. Bladder

b. Penis

c. Epididymis

d. Testes

97

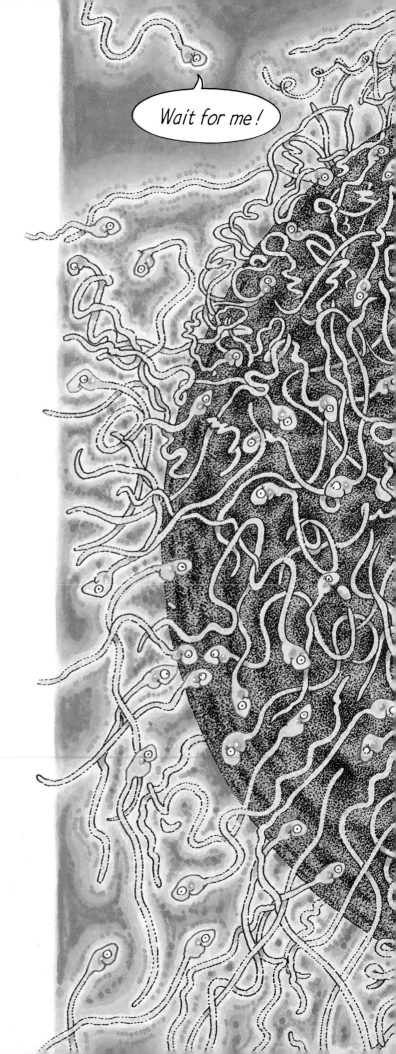

The egg and sperm race is on! Five hundred million sperm are trying to reach the egg. It's quite a journey and only one will win. Sperm are only twenty-four ten-thousandths of an inch long and yet they have to swim for six to ten inches. (This would be like you swimming over one hundred lengths in an Olympic-size swimming pool). Sperm rest for half an hour or so while chemicals in the vagina make them ready for their journey. Then they're off, beating their tails as fast as they can!

Many millions are soon lost in the microscopic crevices and blind alleys of the vagina. Some make it to the neck of the uterus. More trouble lurks there. Defender macrophages and neutrophils attack invading sperm! Up in the uterus, the surviving sperm have to battle against waves of microscopic hairs that try to waft them backwards. On they struggle to the top of the uterus and into the fallopian tube. Now the egg is near. Of the five hundred million sperm that started the journey only a few hundred have survived this far.

The egg is surrounded by thousands of cells that provide food for it. The sperm start fighting through these layers, pushing the cells away. Their beating tails make the egg spin round in a clockwise direction. Suddenly some of them reach the egg cell wall, but just one sperm breaks through. Leaving its tail behind it enters the egg. And in the tiniest fraction of a second, the egg changes so that no more sperm can enter. Something quite remarkable happens …

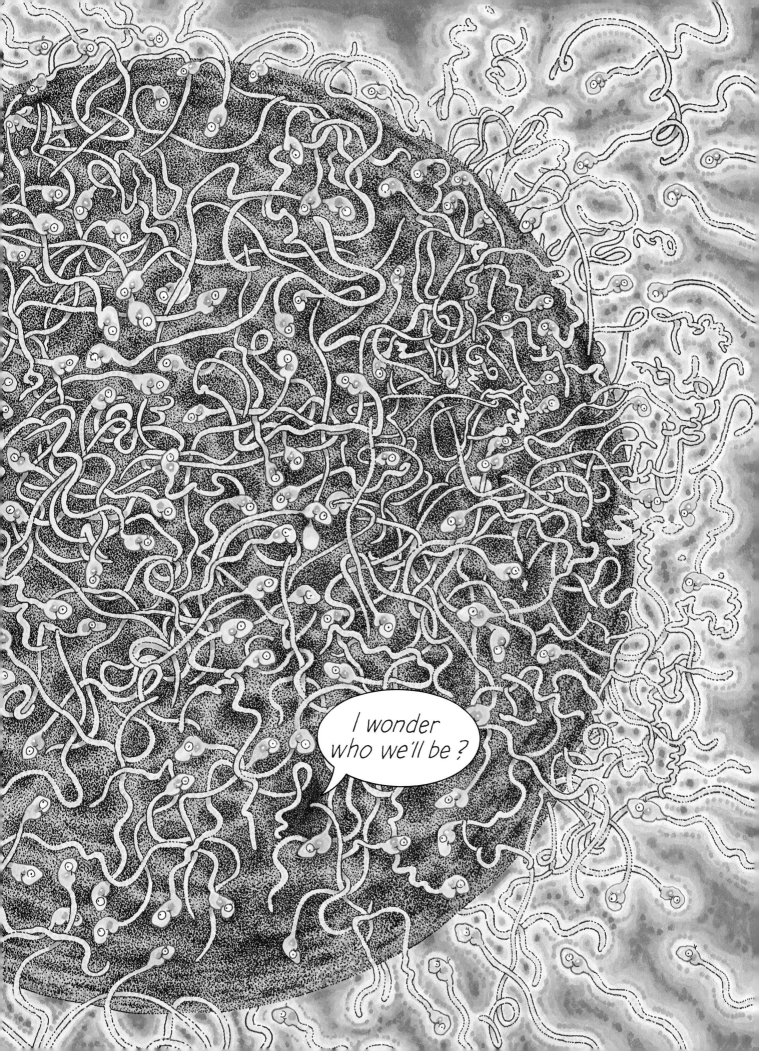

…the process of making a new human being begins. The insides of the new cell swirl vigorously around, as if to force the egg and sperm chromosomes to meet. Very soon, in a matter of hours, the cell copies its DNA and the first cell becomes two cells.

Within twelve hours, those two cells become four cells; twelve hours later those four cells become eight cells, each with identical DNA plans inside them. While all this DNA copying and cell division is going on, the ball of cells is moving slowly down the fallopian tube towards the uterus.

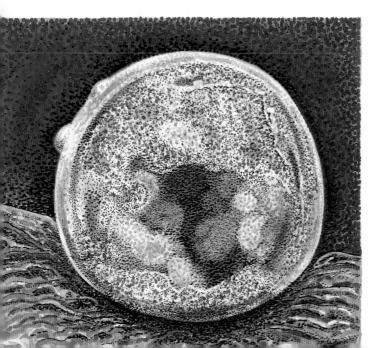

The embryo, now made from about two hundred cells, settles firmly on the wall of the uterus. Already its cells are several different shapes and sizes. What happens next is one of life's greatest marvels and scientific mysteries. Those few cells divide and move and change in a precise order to make all the parts of the human body.

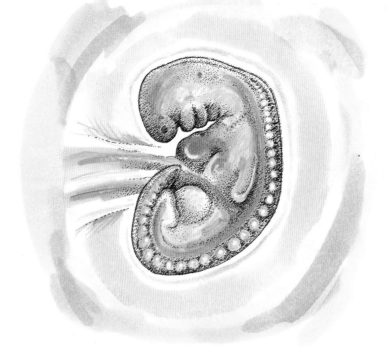

Four weeks after the egg and sperm first met, the embryo is about twenty-eight thousandths of an inch long. It is now enclosed in a fluid-filled sac which keeps it safe and warm. The embryo has a heart that beats irregularly at first, but soon twice as fast as its mother's. The spine and nervous system start to form, but the lower half of its body looks like a pointed tail.

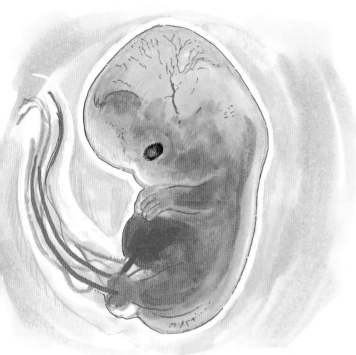

By six weeks, the embryo is just over three-eighths of an inch long. The head has begun to develop, enclosing the beginnings of the brain. The digestive system has almost formed in the last two weeks, and the liver and kidneys are in place but do not work yet. The arms and legs show as little buds and the mouth and jaws are starting to form, with holes where the nostrils will be.

The embryo is now eight weeks old. Its eyes are almost fully developed, the nose its taking shape and tiny fingers and toes bud from the arms and legs. Lungs have formed and the heavy head leans forward over the chest. In just fifty-six days the foundations for every single part of the body have been laid, and yet the embryo is only one and a half inches long – smaller than your little finger!

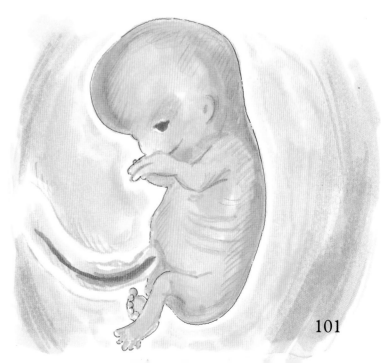

All this growing and moving uses up a
lot of food and oxygen, but the unborn
baby cannot eat or breathe. All food
and oxygen must come from the mother.
Early on, some of its cells formed the
placenta (*pla-sen-ta*), a spongy lump
strongly stuck to the wall of the uterus.
In the placenta many of the baby's blood
vessels lie very close to the mother's
blood vessels. Food and oxygen leak out
from the mother's blood vessels through
the walls of the baby's blood vessels and
waste products leak from the baby to the
mother, but their blood cells never mix.
The placenta also produces hormones
that help the mother's body to change
during pregnancy and get ready for
delivering the baby to the outside world.
The baby is attached to the placenta
by a long cord called the umbilicus
(*um-bill-i-cus*) as a space-walking
astronaut is linked to the spacecraft.

Safe and warm inside the uterus, this
baby really has to grow now! At nine
weeks it weighs just one-quarter ounce
but by the time it is born, about thirty
weeks later, it will probably weigh seven
or eight pounds. Its feet will lengthen
from one quarter inch to over three
inches. The baby slowly begins to explore its
watery world, but the mother cannot feel
it moving until about seventeen weeks.
With every passing week, the face looks
more human, and hair, toenails and
fingernails grow. By twenty-six weeks or
so, the baby's lungs could breathe air,
and it has a chance of surviving if it is
born too early. During the last ten weeks
the baby starts to get quite chubby and its
fingers can grasp.

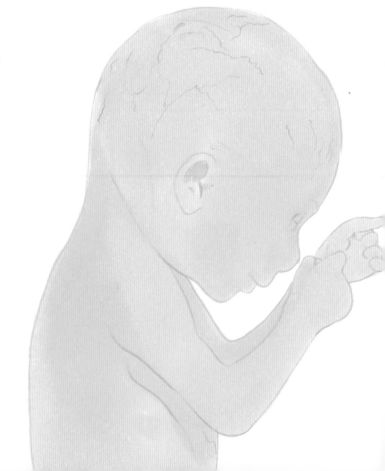

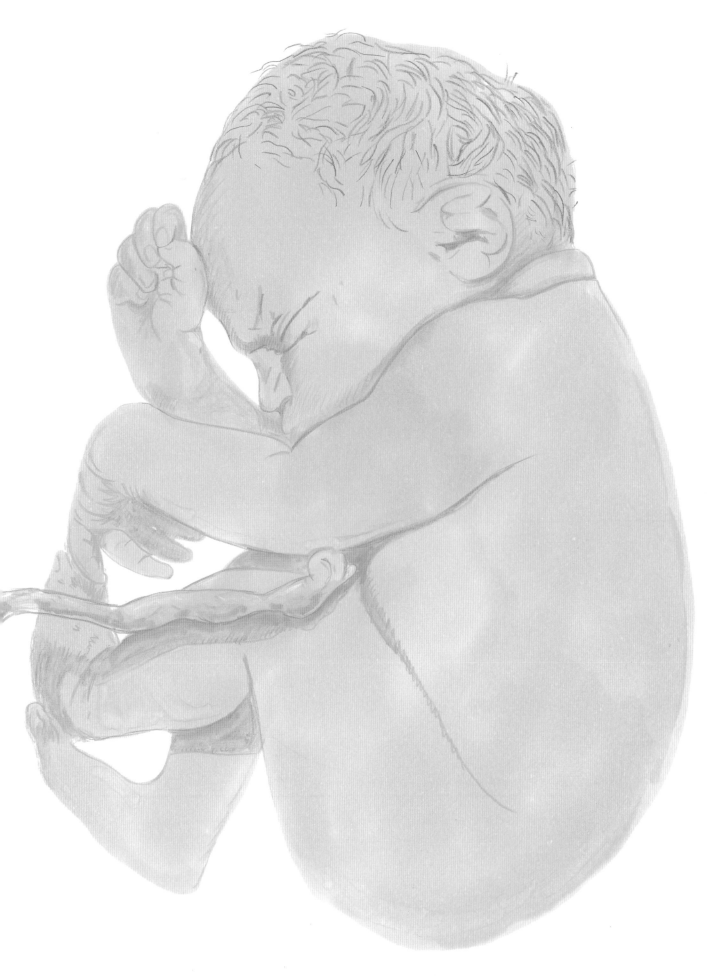

By about forty weeks, the baby is ready to make its journty to the outside world. How will it get there? The neck of the uterus is closed and the vagina is narrow. But the wall of the uterus is made of very strong muscles which start contracting and pushing the baby downwards. Then the neck of the uterus opens and stretches to four inches wide. It is still a tight fit, but there are spaces in the baby's skull bones so that the head can be squeezed through. The vagina is very stretchy and it isn't long before the baby's eyes are looking at their mother for the first time.

Chemical messages, particularly the hormone adrenaline, travel rapidly to the lung cells to tell them to change their job and clear the lungs of salty fluid. Valves separating the two halves of the baby's heart lock into place so that the blood can carry oxygen from the lungs around the body.

The baby takes its first breath, probably lets out a loud cry…

Happy Birthday!

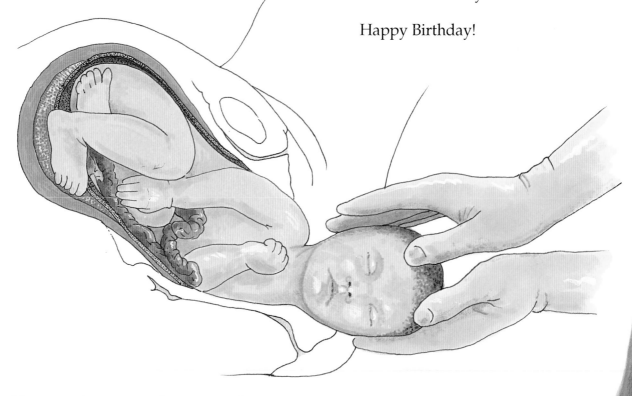

Two very important things must happen in an instant. First, the baby must start breathing air, and second, its blood must change direction. After forty weeks of making fluid, cells lining the lungs must start pumping fluid away, so that the baby can take its first lungful of air.

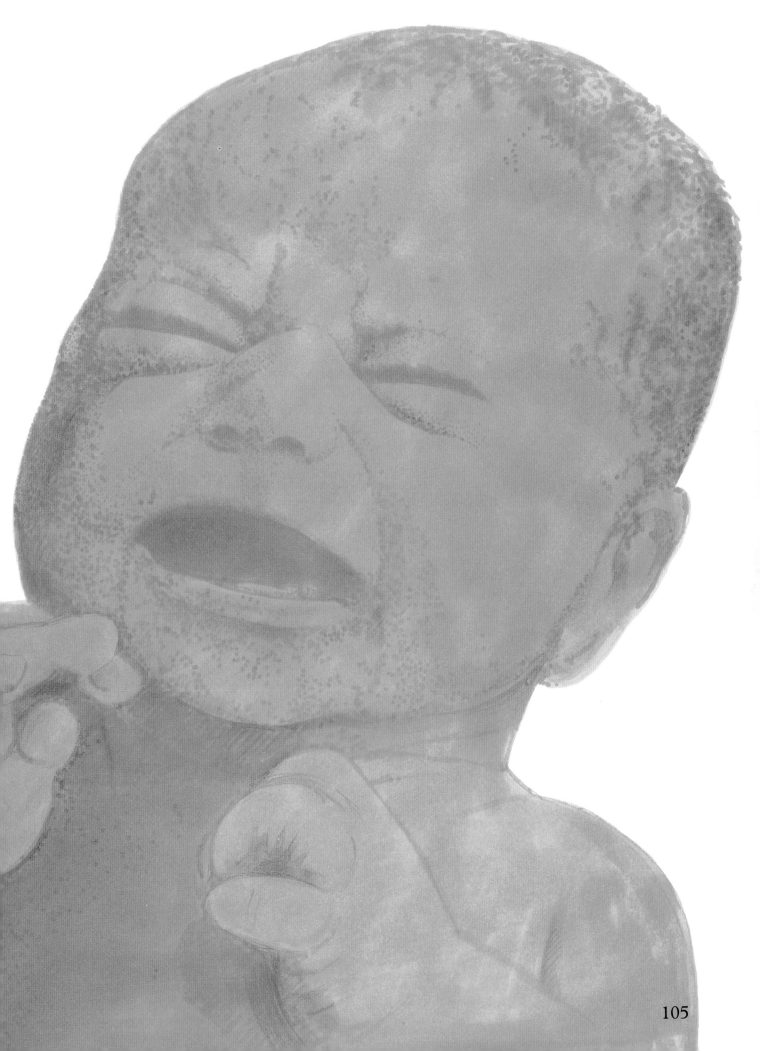

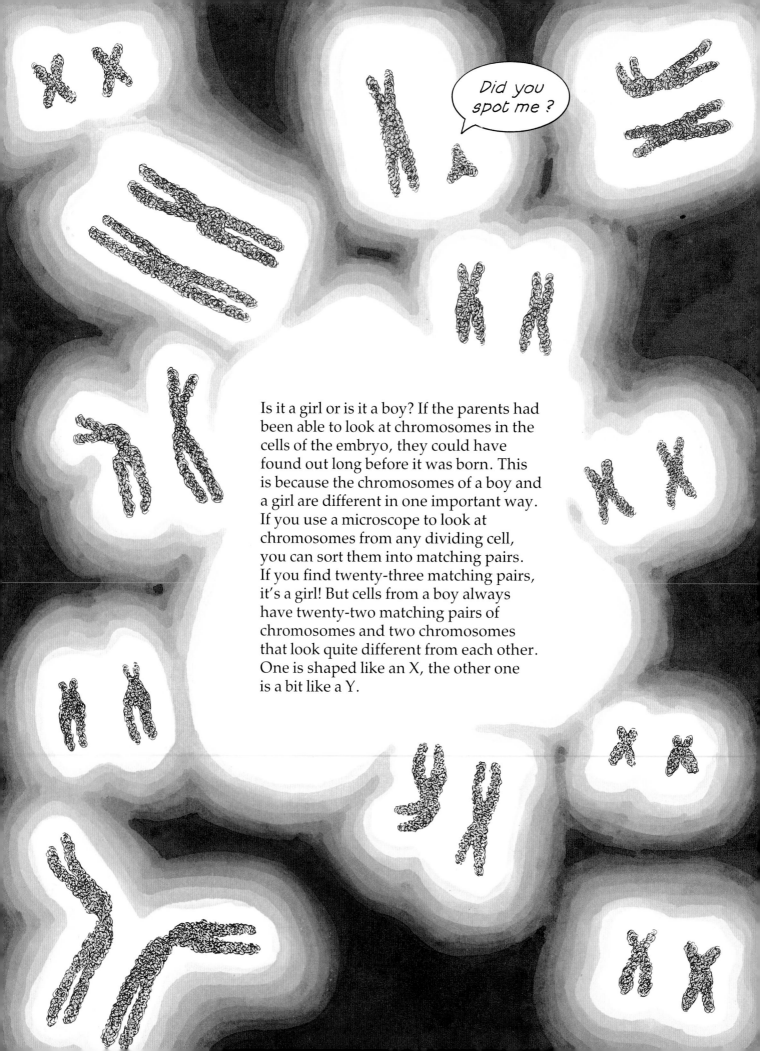

Did you spot me?

Is it a girl or is it a boy? If the parents had been able to look at chromosomes in the cells of the embryo, they could have found out long before it was born. This is because the chromosomes of a boy and a girl are different in one important way. If you use a microscope to look at chromosomes from any dividing cell, you can sort them into matching pairs. If you find twenty-three matching pairs, it's a girl! But cells from a boy always have twenty-two matching pairs of chromosomes and two chromosomes that look quite different from each other. One is shaped like an X, the other one is a bit like a Y.

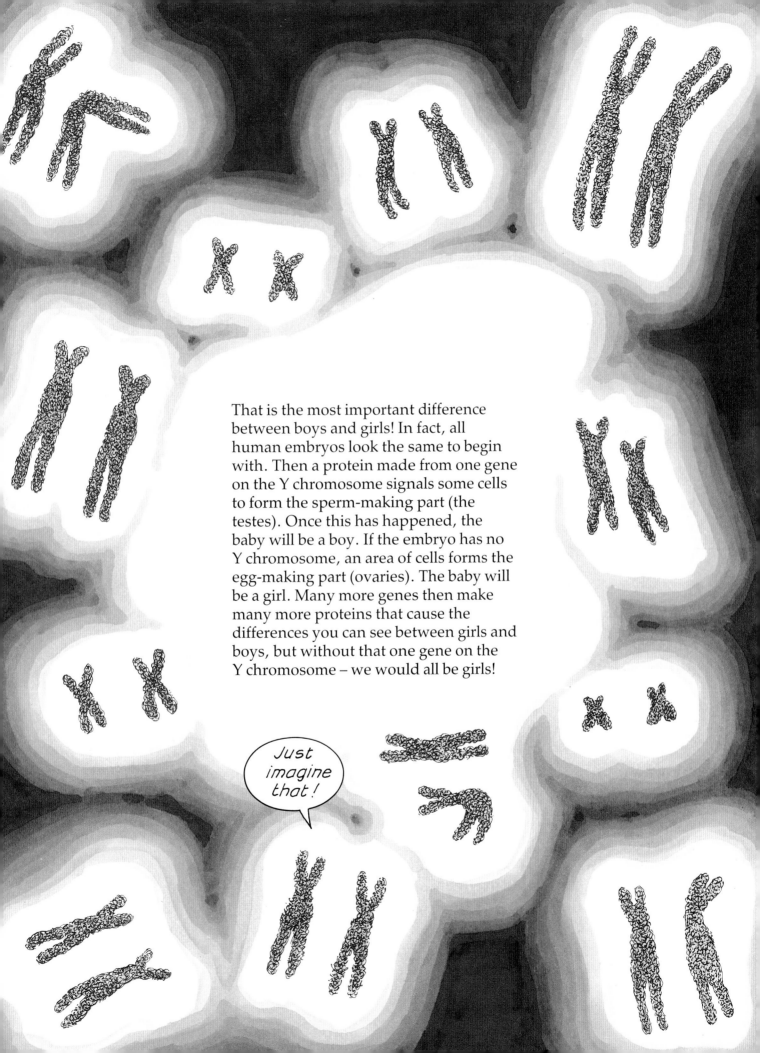

That is the most important difference between boys and girls! In fact, all human embryos look the same to begin with. Then a protein made from one gene on the Y chromosome signals some cells to form the sperm-making part (the testes). Once this has happened, the baby will be a boy. If the embryo has no Y chromosome, an area of cells forms the egg-making part (ovaries). The baby will be a girl. Many more genes then make many more proteins that cause the differences you can see between girls and boys, but without that one gene on the Y chromosome – we would all be girls!

Just imagine that!

We have told you about the incredible growth of a human baby from just one cell. But what happens in other animals is just as miraculous. Can you see how similar we are to fishes, amphibians, reptiles and birds when we are only made of a few million cells! For the first five weeks of life, human embryos are very like other mammals, birds, reptiles and even fish. All these embryos have tails, for instance, and make many of the same parts, although they may use them for different jobs later. You once had a tiny kidney just like a fish has, but your real kidneys were made in another part of your body. Your fish kidney became your ovaries or testes, making eggs or sperm!

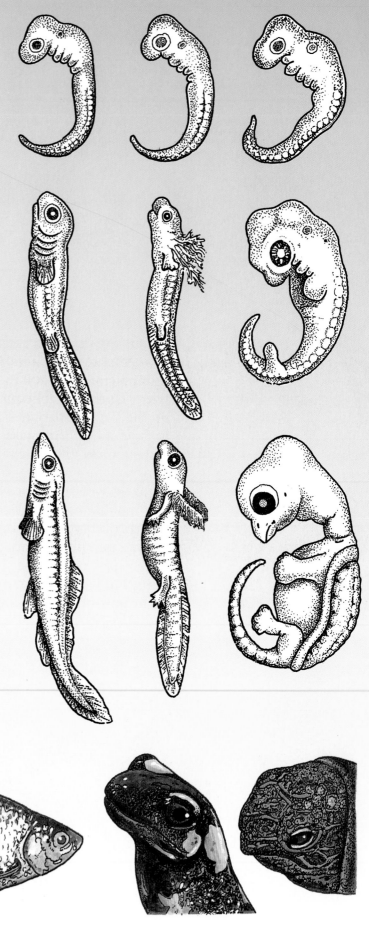

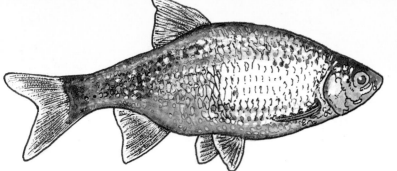

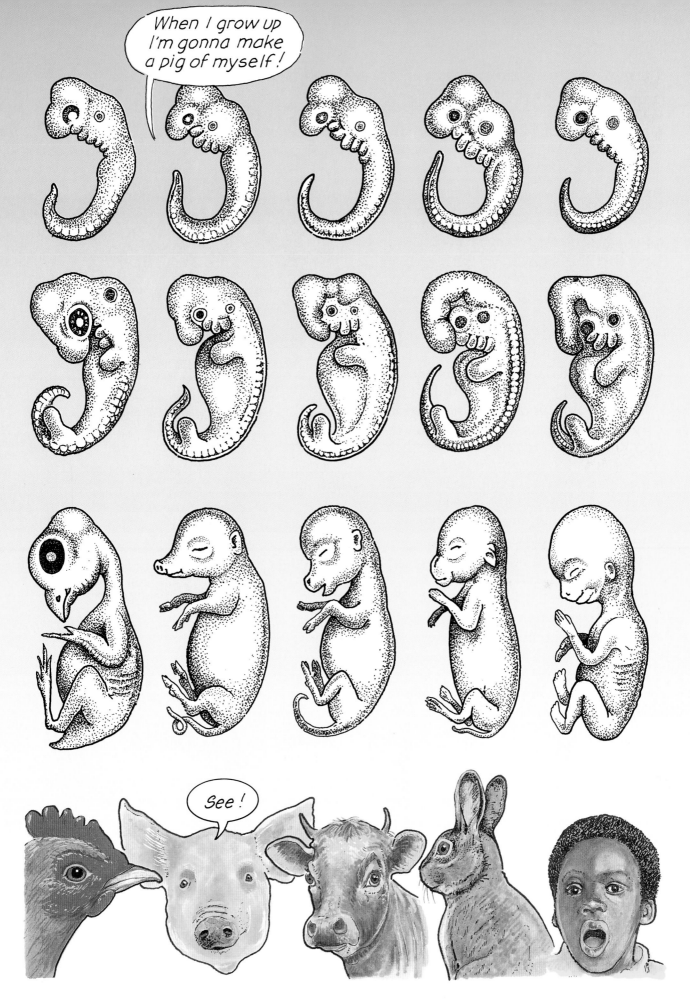

The most important part of making any of the creatures we showed you on the previous page, is that a cell from the father, the sperm, joins with a cell from the mother, the egg, to make a new and unique being. The genes of the mother mix with the genes of the father so that the new creature will have two copies of each one of its genes, one copy from its father and one copy from its mother. How does this happen?

Egg and sperm are always made by a special type of cell division. In humans, for instance, they don't have forty-six chromosomes like all the other cells in the body, they have only twenty-three chromosomes. This means that when the egg and sperm join together, the first cell of the new human being has forty-six chromosomes again, twenty-three from the mother that carry one copy of each of her genes and twenty-three from the father that carry one copy of each of his genes. So there are two to the power of twenty-three different combinations of chromosomes (and therefore genes) possible in each egg or sperm!

But when a new life, be it fish, fowl or flamingo, is made, the new animal will be unique. This is because something extremely clever takes place as sperm and eggs are made in the father's and mother's bodies. We'll show you what happens in human cells.

At the beginning of the egg- or sperm-making process, all the cells have twenty-three pairs of chromosomes. To make it easier to understand we have just drawn two pairs.

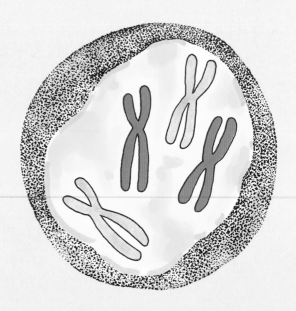

The chromosomes get shorter and fatter as they do when a cell is going to divide.

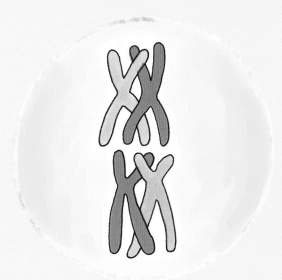

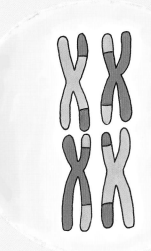

Then they get very close together and begin to wind around each other.

The chromosomes swap some of their genes.

The sperm or egg cells still have twenty-three pairs of chromosomes. But each cell has a completely different mixture of genes from the parent cell.

The sperm or egg cells divide again and this time only one chromosome from each pair goes into each cell. The sperm can meet the egg and create unique new creatures!

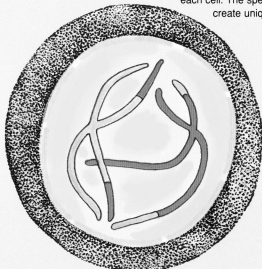
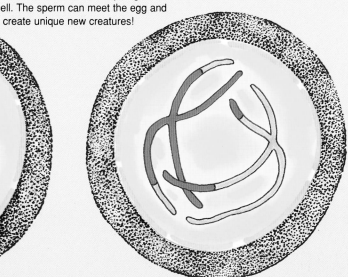

Superhuman?

Congratulations on reading this far. You deserve a little rest. We want you to relax for one minute. If you say one tabby cat, two tabby cats, three tabby cats, and so on, up to sixty tabby cats, about one minute will have passed. Start counting…

While you've been counting, do you know what your body has done? (These are approximate. Exact amounts will depend on your age, size and sex.)

Your heart has beaten about seventy times.

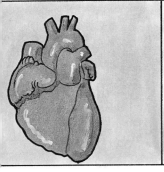

You have shed one thousandth of a gram of dead skin cells.

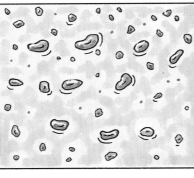

You have taken twenty or so new breaths.

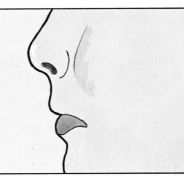

You have rebuilt one thousandth of a gram of bone.

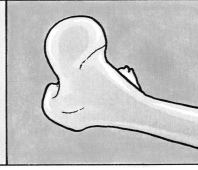

You have made about one sixty-fourth of an ounce of stomach acid.

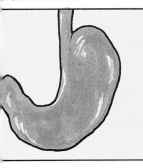

You have made one thirty-second of an ounce of urine.

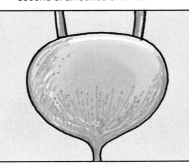

Blood could have gone from your heart to your lungs, to heart, to body, to heart again.

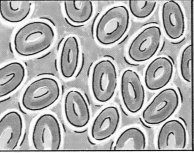

You have made one sixty-fourth of an ounce of saliva.

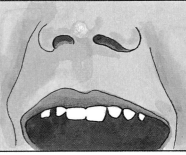

Your liver cells have made about one sixty-fourth of an ounce of bile.

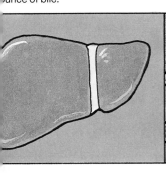

You have made about seven hundred thousand lymphocytes.

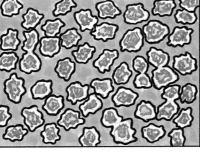

Your heart has pumped two or three quarts of blood.

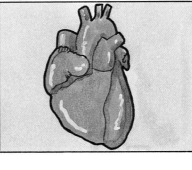

Gases have travelled through your nose at four hundred and thirty-six feet per minute.

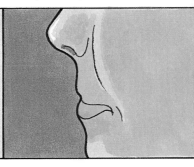

Your brain has used a quarter of a cubic inch of oxygen for energy.

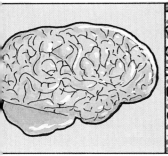

You have made about six hundred million platelets.

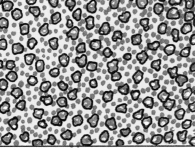

You have breathed in five or six quarts of air.

You will have absorbed about a tenth of an ounce of water in your intestines.

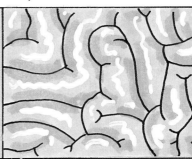

You have made about eighty million new neutrophils.

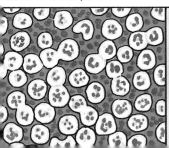

Your kidneys have filtered about five sixths of an ounce of blood.

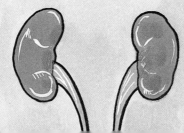

Your liver has filtered one quart of blood.

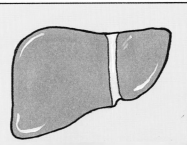

You have breathed out about a hundred cubic inches of carbon dioxide.

Blood in your veins could have travelled forty feet.

Your brain has used about two ounces of glucose for energy.

You have lost two hundredths of an ounce of sweat – or more!

Blood in your arteries could have travelled one hundred feet.

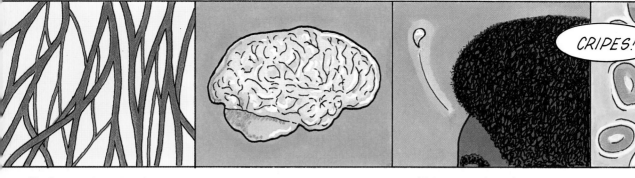

You have made one hundredth of an ounce of mucus up your nose.

You will have lost about six hundred million platelets.

Three waves of muscle contractions have moved across your stomach.

You have breathed about eighty-four cubic inches of carbon dioxide.

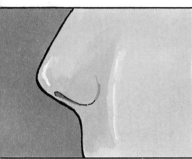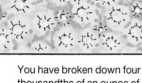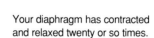

You have made about three hundred million new red blood cells.

You have broken down four thousandths of an ounce of bone.

Your diaphragm has contracted and relaxed twenty or so times.

You have replaced about one five–thousandth of the cells lining your intestines.

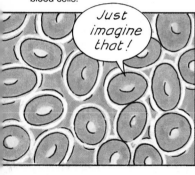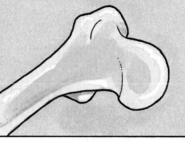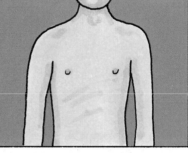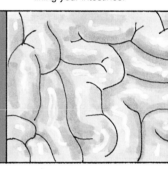

You have consumed about nine cubic inches of oxygen.

You have made about one thirty–second of an ounce of fluid that helps your intestine digest food.

Your brain has used one fifth of the energy your body has made in one minute.

The hair on your head has grown two thousandths of an inch.

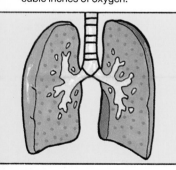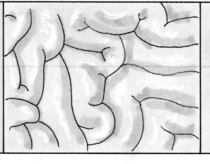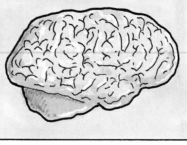

Food has travelled one inch in your large intestine.

Blood in your capillaries has travelled seven inches.

About three hundred million of your red blood cells have died.

Your fingernails have grown about four ten–thousandths of an inch.

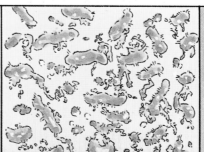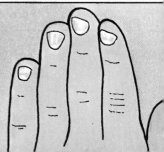

You have blinked at least [fi]ve times.

You may have coughed to remove irritating particles in your lungs.

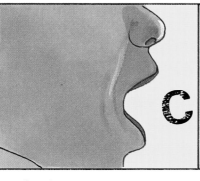

Coughed-out air would go as fast as ten miles per minute.

Your blood cells have absorbed about twelve cubic inches of oxygen from your lungs.

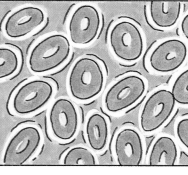

[Y]ou may have yawned [b]ecause of excess carbon [d]ioxide – or boredom!

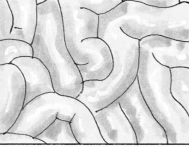

Intestine muscle contractions will have travelled forty-seven inches.

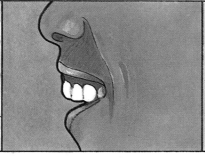

Your body has lost in total about a thirty – second of an ounce of water.

You have made about one three-hundredth of an ounce of mucus in your breathing tubes.

YUK!

[A]bout seven hundred thousand [o]f your lymphocytes have died.

ZAP!

ZAP!

You have breathed in about one quart of oxygen.

You have burnt up about three foot-pounds of food energy.

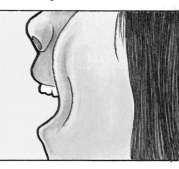

You may have sneezed to blow out dust, germs, and mucus.

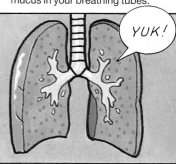

[N]erve signals could travel [f]our miles along an axon [if] you had one that long!).

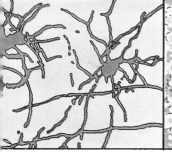

About eighty million neutrophils have died.

Bye!

You will have lost about one five – thousandth of the cells lining your intestines.

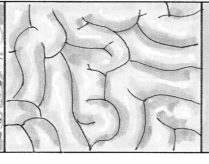

Your toenails have grown about four ten–thousandths of an inch.

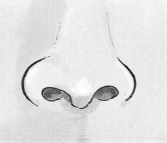

Phew!

[Y]our heart has used thirty–five [h]undredths of an ounce of [g]lucose for energy.

You have renewed two hundred thousandths of your total skin area.

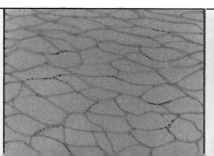

You have breathed in and out about four quarts of nitrogen.

WE CAN'T THINK OF ANY MORE – CAN YOU ?

Maybe you can now appreciate the wonderful ways your cells work together to make the incredibly sophisticated and complicated machine that is your body.

Many other animals have bodies that work in much the same way as yours; whales and elephants have more cells than you, and all of them have DNA plans. But none of them would be able to read and understand this book. Animals may be able to communicate with each other in many ways, but they cannot speak to each other from opposite sides of the world, or from a space station back to Earth.

$$E = mc^2$$

If you give a chimpanzee a paintbrush and paint, it may make some interesting splotches, but no other animal could draw pictures like those on this page, or create the famous paintings and sculptures that you see in art galleries. No animal farms for its food as we do, or can cure its injured or sick as well as we can, and none has been as successful in populating every corner of the planet. Humans may behave like animals in many ways, but in the last fifty thousand years we have developed skills in exploring and understanding the world around us that make us unique in the history of the planet.

However…

…there are other aspects of human behavior that are not so useful. Our destructiveness, for example. As far as we can tell no other animal has ever caused so much damage to the living Earth. Many millions of plants and animals that existed as little as fifty years ago will never be seen by your children or grandchildren. Many beautiful landscapes have been wrecked. Chemical pollution threatens our climate, our rivers and seas, the air that we breathe, and the food that we eat. The same skills and intelligence that allow us to make computers, spacecraft, to cure diseases and to cultivate our land, also give us the means to destroy the planet. Few animals wage such total war against their own species and cause so much suffering to thousands of innocent victims.

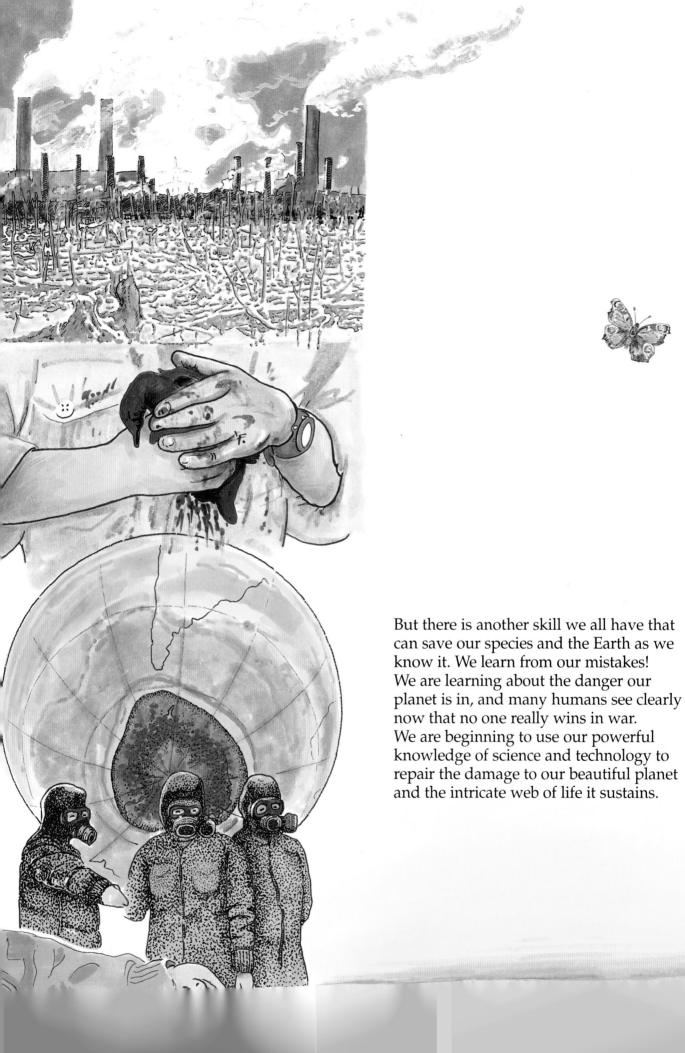

But there is another skill we all have that
can save our species and the Earth as we
know it. We learn from our mistakes!
We are learning about the danger our
planet is in, and many humans see clearly
now that no one really wins in war.
We are beginning to use our powerful
knowledge of science and technology to
repair the damage to our beautiful planet
and the intricate web of life it sustains.

These good and bad aspects of our species set us apart from all other forms of life on this planet. Other animals undoubtedly possess some of our skills and bad habits, but none have developed them to the level of human beings. Yet the amazing fact is that less than two percent of our DNA is different from our nearest relatives, the chimpanzees.

If human beings are unique in the animal kingdom and the history of planet Earth, what about the rest of the universe? There are probably millions of suns that have solar systems like ours. Somewhere out in deep space, the conditions may be right to make DNA, proteins, and the other complicated chemicals necessary for life.

Every minute of every day scientists scan the skies for radio signals from the stars, in the hope that other forms of intelligent life might be trying to contact us.

But what would we do if we did receive a message?

Index and Glossary

Page numbers in **bold** type indicate major references

cell membrane the perimeter fence of a cell, made of fats and proteins. Controls what passes in and out of cell and sends chemical messages to and from other cells   12, 27, 83

centimeter a unit of measurement. One hundredth of a meter, about three-eighths of an inch.

cerebellum (*ser-ee-bell-um*) part of the brain that coordinates muscles and balance   69

cerebral cortex (*ser-ee-brall cor-tex*) part of the brain that handles messages from your five senses, controls complicated movements, the ability to paint pictures, play musical instruments, understand speech and language, write stories, solve puzzles, conscious thought and memory   69

chicken pox common virus infection, usually in children. Causes itchy spots and fever and patient normally gets better within a few days   87, 88, 89

chimpanzee closest animal relative of human beings   41, 117, 120

chondrocyte (*con-dro-site*) cartilage-making cell   90

chromosomes (*krome-oh-soames*) thin strands of DNA found in the nuclei of cells. Before a cell divides they become shorter and fatter. Human beings have 46 chromosomes   29, 31, 32, 33, 36, 100, **106**, **107**, **110–111**

clot plug of fibers, platelets and red blood cells that seals a wound   46, 90

collagen (*coll-a-jen*) tough protein found in skin and bone   42, 49, 60, 91

comet small object that orbits the sun and contains a lot of ice. When comet enters solar system the sun burns up the icy material and a glowing tail can sometimes be seen from Earth   9, 11, 16

cone cells cells in retina that are triggered by colored light, and send signals to the brain   71

coral invertebrate creatures that grow in enormous colonies made from hundreds of different species to form coral reefs   13

cornea transparent window at front of eye that forms its first lens   70

crocodiles reptiles that are the largest air breathing fresh water carnivores. Creatures like these have been on Earth since the age of the dinosaurs   16

cyokines (*sye-toe-kines*) messenger molecules of defender cells   83, 87, 89

cytoplasm (*sye-toe-plas-em*) clear liquid inside a cell surrounding everything else that is there   27, 32, 37, 66

cytosine (*sye-toe-seen*), **C**, one of the four chemicals that make the DNA code   30, 31, 40

D

defender cells name we use in this book for cells in the body that fight disease. Neutrophils, macrophages and lymphocytes are defender cells   46, 54, 60, **78–91**, 113, 114, 115

dendrites (*den-drites*) fine branches on one side of a nerve cell that receive information and turn it into an electrical signal   66, 71

dentine (*den-teen*) hard substance made by odontoblast cells in the tooth. Made of calcium, phosphorus, and a protein scaffolding   61

dermis (*der-miss*) middle layer of skin that contains tiny blood vessels, nerve cells, hair follicles, sweat and oil making cells in a tough elastic jelly made of collagen   42

diaphragm (*die-a fram*) a powerful muscle under your lungs that contracts and expands as you breathe   51, 56

digestive system a long and twisting food processing tube that digests your food. Main parts are mouth, esophagus, stomach, small intestine, large intestine, rectum and anus   **52-55**, 68, 101

dinosaurs kings of the reptiles, dominated the earth for 120 million years   15, 16

DNA deoxyribonucleic acid (*dee-oxy-rye-bow-new-clee-ick acid*): the chemical plans in each of your cells that make you unique, and control the way your cells behave   **28-41**, 44, 92, 10

double helix name for the shape of DNA. Two spirals twisting round each other   29, 30

E

ear organ of body that channels and receives sound waves and transmits them as electrical signals to the brain   34, 66, 68, **74–75**

eardrum thin partition of fibrous tissue between outer ear and middle ear, that vibrates when hit by sound waves   74

earth your home planet   **9–11**, 13, 15

earthquake natural disaster resulting from movements under the Earth's rocky surface   10

egg cell from the mother that joins with a sperm to make a new human being   19, 96, 98, 100, 110–111

electron microscope a very powerful microscope that can magnify more than ten thousand times   20, 22, 24, 26, 29, 31

embryo unborn creature made of just a few cells. A developing human baby is called an embryo for the first eight weeks after fertilization   **100-101**, 106, 107, 108

enamel hard substance on the outside of teeth. Made of calcium, phosphorus, and protein by ameloblast cells   61

environment surroundings, surrounding objects or conditions of life   16, 41

enzymes (*en-zimes*) proteins that digest or break other substances into smaller and more simple substances   52, 54

epididymis (*ep-ee-did-ee-mis*) place in the testes where sperm are stored   96, 97

esophagus (*ee-sof-ag-us*) short thick tube that pushes food into your stomach. Part of your digestive system   52, 54

evolution development of all the many forms of life

on Earth today by change from earlier forms of life   16, 40, 41

evolve   to change and develop by natural processes, as bacteria and algae evolved into the millions of different life forms on Earth today   40, 41

extinction   total loss of a species   16

eye   organ of body that collects light waves, focuses them and sends electrical signals to the brain giving sight   34, 66, 68, **70–71**, 75, 101

F

fallopian tube   (*fal-oh-pee-an*) egg catching tube, attached to the uterus. The place where the sperm first meets the egg   96, 97, 98, 100

fat   substances that are an essential part of our diet. Turned by the body into energy stores. A fat cell layer beneath the skin acts as a shock absorber and keeps you warm   23, 24, 34, 42, 52, 53, 55, 57,

fetus   unborn creature, larger than an embryo. In humans from eight weeks after fertilization to birth **102, 103**

fibroblasts   (*fye-bro-blasts*) cells that repair damage in the body   61, 89, 90, 91

finger   you know you have ten, but did you know that each one is made of about ten thousand million cells, and has two or three bones?   21, 22, 23, 34

fingernails   plate of tightly packed cells making keratin that protects ends of fingers and helps you grasp and manipulate small objects   23, 41, 45, 102

fish   cold blooded vertebrate animal living in water with fins, gills, and a scaly skin   14

food chain   systems of living creatures interrelated in their feeding habits, the smallest being eaten by the larger which are in turn eaten by still larger ones. Humans depend on two kinds of food chains or webs to obtain energy and materials necessary for life. One is based in the seas, the other on land   84

fungus   (plural fungi) plant without the green pigment chlorophyll eg, mushroom, toadstool, moulds. Some types of fungus can occasionally cause disease in humans   87

G

galaxy,   an enormous collection of stars bound together by gravity. Earth's star, the sun, belongs to a spiral galaxy called the Milky Way   8, 20

gene   DNA recipe for making a protein   34, 36, 39, 40, 107, 110, 111

germ   in this book the word germ means microscopic creature that can cause disease   78, 80, 81, 82

glomeruli   (*glom-e-rule-aye*) knots of tiny blood vessels with very thin walls. Blood is filtered from these into the kidney   59

glucose   simple sugar broken down in cells to produce energy   114, 115

glycogen   (*glye-co-jen*) energy store found in liver cells   27

gram   a unit of weight. There are one thousand grams in a kilogram

gravity   an important force of nature that is responsible for the motion of falling objects to the Earth's surface, weight of objects, tides and the orbits of planets   4

guanine   (*gwa-neen*), **G**, one of the four chemicals that make the DNA code   30, 31, 40

H

hair   hollow tube made of keratin protein   23, 34, 42, 45, 102, 113

hair follicle   (*fol-ik-all*) found in skin. Each follicle is a factory for making one hair   45, 62

heart   fist sized muscular pump that circulates blood around the body   48, **49**, 62, 68, 93, 101, 104, 113, 114, 115

hemoglobin   (*heem-o-glow-bin*) protein in red blood cells that carries oxygen around the body   46

hepatocyte   (*hep-at-o-site*) large cell in the liver that processes foods, renders poisons and body waste harmless, and makes bile   56

Homo sapiens   (*sap-ee-ens*) scientific term for human species   17

hormones   (*hor-moans*) chemical messages produced by cells that change the way other cells work   46, 94, 95, 96, 102

hypothalamus   (*high-po-thal-am-us*) part of the brain that maintains a constant internal environment   69

I

ice age   long range changes in Earth's climate when enormous ice sheets advance from polar regions   16

intestine   very long coiled muscular tube where most of your food is digested. It is about 20 feet long   48, 56, 62, 113, 114, 115

invertebrates   (*in-vert-ee-brates*) ainmals without a backbone e.g. jellyfish and insects   13

iris   colored part of the eye. It has a hole in the center called the pupil which controls the amount of light entering the eye by getting larger or smaller   70

J

jellyfish   a sea animal without a backbone that has a clear soft body and tentacles   13

joint   place where two bones meet   65, 66

K

keratin   (*kera-tin*) tough protein made by skin cells   42, 45

kidneys   important organs that filter out harmful substances from your blood, and keep the fluid balance in your body   58–59, 94, 101, 113

killer cells   defender cells that seek out and destroy cells infected with viruses   83, 87

kilogram   a unit of weight that is equal to one thousand grams.

kilometer   a unit of measurement, one thousand meters.

L

large intestine part of the digestive system containing the solid waste products of digestion. Water, bacteria, undigested proteins, fats and plant material move slowly through and water is absorbed 53, 55

larynx a cavity in the throat that contains the vocal cords (also called voice box) 96

lens (of the eye) transparent structure made of layers of proteins called crystallines. Fine tunes focusing of light rays for clear sight 70

liver important organ that is the chemical processing plant of your body. Liver cells make bile that helps digestion of fat; process products of food digestion in blood into substances the body really needs; break down harmful substances; clear blood of bacteria, and recycle dead and dying blood cells 24, **56–57**, 58, 101, 113

lungs large spongy organs in your chest where oxygen gets into your body and carbon dioxide is released 48, 49, **50–51**, 68, 78, 81, 101, 102, 104

lymph (*limf*) watery fluid that flows in the lymph vessels 48

lymph nodes part of lymphatic system. Oval or bean shaped structures located along length of lymphatic system. Contain many defender cells 48, 88

lymphatic system (*lim-fat-ick*) lymph vessels and lymph nodes carry fluid around the body. Involved in dealing with waste, germs, and excess fluid in the tissues **48**, 88

lymphocytes (*lim-fo-sites*) defender cells that can make special weapons called antibodies or turn into killer cells 79, 81, 82, 83, 88, 89, 113, 114

lysosomes (*lye-so-soames*) small bags of chemicals inside cells that digest rubbish and germs from inside and outside the cell 27

M

macrophages (*mac-ro-fay-jes*) defender cells that eat up germs and rubbish and help lymphocytes 56, 79, 81, 82, 83, 88, 90, 98

mammal vertebrate animal, usually four legged with body hair, that gives birth to live young and nourishes them with mother's milk 15, 16

melanin (*mella-nin*) protein pigment that gives your skin its color and protects you from harmful sun rays 44, 71

melanocyte (*mel-an-oh-sites*) a cell that makes the protein pigment melanin 44

membrane of cell the perimeter fence of a cell, made of fats and proteins. Controls what passes in and out of cell and sends chemical messages to and from other cells 12, 27, 83

menstruation (*men-strew-a-shon*) shedding of the lining of the uterus if the egg is not fertilized 96

meteorite small object, often remains of comet, that travels through space and collides with the Earth 11, 15, 16

microscope a magnifying machine that lets you see cells close up 20, 46, 54

millimeter a measure of length, one thousandth of a meter, about four thousandths of an inch.

million one thousand thousand

mitochondrion (*mye-toe-con-dre-on*) (plural mitochondria) power station inside your cells that makes, supplies and stores energy 26, 49

molecule two or more atoms combined by a chemical reaction. The smallest physical unit of any compound. For instance, a molecule of water is two atoms of hydrogen and one of oxygen.

moon Earth's satellite 9

mouth cavity formed by cheeks, hard and soft palates and the tongue 34, 52, 66, 68, 77, 101

mucus (*mew-cus*) gloppy liquid produced in your body to trap germs 55, 76, 78, 114, 115

muscles make your body move. Made of millions of muscle cells, with nerves that control them. Three main types, cardiac, smooth and skeletal or striped 16, 49, 54, **62–65**, 66, 68, 69, 95, 104

mutation (*mew-tay-shon*) mistake in the DNA chemical plans in a cell 41

myosin (*my-oh-sin*) slick protein in muscle cells that helps them contract and expand 63

N

nails plates of tightly packed cells making keratin that protect ends of fingers and toes and help your fingers grasp and manipulate small objects 23, 34, 41, 45, 102, 114

nautiloid ancestor of the modern octopus, with many tentacles, keen eyes and a tough protective shell 13

nephron (*nef-ron*) collecting tube in the kidneys 59

nerve a bundle of milions of nerve cell axons plus blood vessels and protective insulating cells and fibers 42, 60, 61, 63, **66**, **67**, 68, 69, 70, 74, 95

nervous system network of nerves that spreads around the body **66–69**, 101

neutrophils (*new-tro-fils*) defender cells that destroy germs by taking them inside the cell and destroying them with chemicals 78, 80, 81, 82, 83, 89, 90, 98, 113, 115

nitrogen a colorless, odorless gas that makes up 78% of the Earth's atmosphere. Nitrogen is also present in animals and plants and is important part of proteins 84

noradrenaline a hormone made by the adrenal gland that prepares the body for the extra effort it has to make when you are in danger, stressed, or carrying out a difficult task. Known as a "fight or flight" hormone 94, 95

nose allows you to breathe and smell, hairy inside surface removes dust, dirt and germs that you breathe in   34, 51, 66, 68, 76, 78, 88, 101, 114

nucleus (*new-clee-us*) (plural nuclei) command center of each cell, where chromosomes are   26, 29, 32, 36

nucleus acids (*new-clee-ick* acids) DNA and RNA are nucleic acids. They are chemicals that contain the instructions for life   24, 34, 52

O

odontoblast (*o-don-toe-blast*) cell in teeth that makes dentine   61

olfactory cells (*oll-factory*) cells with hairy projections found up the nose, in a small area just under the brain. They are triggered by complex gases given off by smelly substances to send electrical messages to the brain   76

optic nerve every light sensitive rod and cone cell of the retina is connected by a nerve to the brain. All these nerve fibers in each eye collect together to form the right or left optic nerves that run back from the eyeball to the brain   70, 71

osteoblast (*os-tee-o-blast*) bone making cell   60, 90, 91

osteoclast (*os-tee-o-clast*) bone destroying cell   60, 91

osteocyte (*os-tee-o-site*) cell that keeps bone healthy   60

ovary (*oav-a-ree*) part of the body that makes and releases eggs in female. Human females have two almond-shaped ovaries that are about three eighths of an inch long and twelve thousandths of an inch wide   96, 97, 107

oxygen (*ox-ee-jen*) gas that is essential to life. Carried by red cells around the body. Used for making energy   12, 14, 34, 46, 48, 50, 51, 102, 113, 114

P

pain receptor ends of nerves found in almost every tissue in the body that respond to any stimulus that is likely to cause damage, for instance intense heat, cold, or pressure   42, 68

parasite animal, plant or single celled creature that lives directly on another animal or plant and relies on it for food   23

pelvic muscles pelvis is another word for hip, so pelvic muscles are all those in the hip region   96

penis sex organ of the male, used for urinating and planting sperm in vagina of female   96, 97

permanent teeth the 32 teeth that appear from 6-17 years of age to replace the 20 baby teeth   61

peroxisomes (*per-oxy-soames*) tiny structures found in cells that destroy harmful substances the cell makes while doing its work   27

placenta (*pla-sen-ta*) tissue made by the embryo that lets it take food from its mother   102

planets objects in space that are smaller than stars and orbit around stars. They shine by reflected light. Can be rocky, like Earth, or made of gas, like Saturn   9

plasma (*plaz-ma*) the fluid part of blood, a clear pale yellow liquid in which many important proteins are dissolved   46

platelets tiny bits of cells that are found in blood and help blood to clot   46, 90

proteins (*prot-eens*) complicated substances made from amino acid building blocks in cells. Proteins make cells the size and shape they are. Proteins help the cell do many of the jobs it has to do   24, **34–41**, 42, 46, 52, 53, 55, 78, 91, 107, 119

pulp (of teeth) tissue containing blood vessels, nerve and lymphatic vessels inside the teeth   61

R

rectum end portion of the digestive system where waste made of water, bacteria, and undigested protein, fats, and plant material, is stored   53

red blood cells small cells in blood that are filled with hemoglobin and carry oxygen around the body   46, 50, 58, 60, 114

reptile a cold blooded vertebrate animal that can live on land, has a scaly skin and lays eggs   15

retina light sensitive layer of cells on the inside of the eye. The cells that respond to light in the retina are the rod and cone cells. They are attached to nerves that transmit signals to the brain   70, 71

ribosomes (*rye-bow-soames*) microscopic protein-making factories found inside cells. The gene recipe is read at the ribosome and new proteins are made. Each of your cells has about ten million ribosomes inside it   26, 36, 37

RNA ribonucleic acid. The messenger strand that carries the DNA recipe for a protein to a ribosome   36, 37

rod cells cells in retina of eye that respond to black and white and dim light and send signals to the brain   71

S

salamander amphibian with a tail and four legs that spends part of its life on water, but leaves the water when the breeding season is over   14

saliva a watery secretion of mucus and fluid produced by glands in the face and neck. Saliva contains enzymes that start digestion, and substances that help kill germs   52, 77, 78

satellite a body that orbits around a planet. The moon is Earth's natural satellite, but man-made satellites also orbit our planet   9

sex hormones hormones produced mainly by the testes and ovaries responsible for changes to a child's body as it grows up. Responsible for many of the physical differences between the male and female body   96

skeleton name given to all the bones that make up the body 60

skin one of the largest organs in the body. In adults the skin covers almost twenty-two square feet and weighs between eight and ten pounds. Skin helps in controlling body temperature and protects the body from water, radiation germs and sharp objects 23, 34, **42-45**, 65, 66, 84, 89, 90, 91, 95, 113, 115

small intestine part of the digestive system after the stomach. About twenty feet long in an adult. The main part of food digestion and absorption happens here. 52, 55, 68

smooth muscles also called involuntary muscles. Not under conscious control of brain but move automatically as in the digestive system 62

solar system name given to the sun, and the planets, asteroids, and satellites that orbit around it 120

species a group of plants or animals whose members have the same characteristics and are able to breed with each other 16, 17, 41

sperm tiny cell with a long tail produced by the male that fertilizes the egg produced by the female 19, 96, 98, 100, 110-111

star object in the universe that generates energy by nuclear fusion, makes light and therefore shines. The sun is a star. Other objects in space like planets shine because they reflect light from stars 8, 20

stomach part of the digestive system, a J-shaped muscular bag that churns up the food and mixes it with acid and enzymes 52, 54, 78, 113, 114

striped muscles make up 40% of body weight. These muscles are responsible for all forms of movement that move bones and joints and are under conscious or voluntary control (also called striated or voluntary or skeletal muscles) 62

subcutaneous layer the bottom layer of skin that contains many fat cells and nerves that are sensitive to touch and pain 42

sun the nearest star to Earth, a ball of glowing gases over a million times larger than Earth, with a temperature of about 27,000°F at its center. The sun's light provides the energy for life on Earth 8, 9, 10

sweat produced by sweat glands in the skin. Mixture of water, salts, sugar and some waste products. Main function of sweat is to help control body temperature. As sweat evaporates a lot of heat is lost from the body 23, 42

T

taste buds group of up to 25 taste cells that respond to chemicals in food and send electrical messages to the brain. About 9,000 taste buds found in tongue 77

teeth hard bone-like structures implanted in the sockets of your jaws 34, **61**, 84

telescope instrument made of lenses and mirrors that can make distant objects appear nearer and larger 20

tendons strong rope-like structures of connective tissue that join muscles to bone 65

testes the parts of the male where sperm and hormones are made 96, 97, 107

thymine (*thy-meen*) **T** one of the four chemicals that make up the DNA code 30, 31, 40

toenails plates of tightly packed cells making keratin that protect ends of toes. 34, 45, 102

tongue triangular shaped tissue attached to lower jaw. Molds food into a ball and sends taste sensations to brain 17, 76, 77

tonsils group of many lymph nodes at back of mouth and in neck. Important in protecting your body from germs that you eat or breathe in 48, 75

touch receptor end of a nerve that responds to pressure 42, 68

trachea (*tray-kee-uh*) (also called windpipe) passageway for air about five inches long and about one inch wide in adults. It is strengthened by incomplete rings of cartilage and divides into the right and left brochi which branch into the lungs 50

triceps muscle that moves the arm 64

trilobites ancestors of insects and spiders 13

U

umbilicus (*um-bill-i-cus*) cord that anchors baby to the placenta in the uterus and through which the baby's blood vessels pass to and from the placenta 102

universe everything that exists, all the millions and millions of galaxies, stars, planets, asteroids and spaces and undetectable objects between them. Current theory is that the universe began about fifteen billion years ago in a raging explosion of unbelievably enormous power and energy. At this stage the universe contained all space and time but was smaller than an atom. It began to expand and continues to expand 7, 8

ureter (*you-reet-er*) tube through which urine passes from kidneys to bladder 58, 59

urine waste liquid produced by the kidneys 58, 59, 113

uterus (*you-ter-us*) pear shaped muscular bag inside a woman's body where a baby grows from a tiny ball of cells (also known as the womb) 96, 97, 98, 100, 102, 104

V

vagina (*vaj-ine-a*) muscular tube that leads from the uterus 96, 97, 98

veins (*vanes*) muscular tubes that bring blood from the tissues back to the heart 48, 114

ventricle (*ven-trick-alls*) one of two pumping

chambers of heart. Receives blood from auricle. Left ventricle pumps blood to body, right ventricle pumps blood to lungs 49

vertebrate (*vert-ee-brate*) animal with a backbone, i.e. fish, amphibian, reptile, bird, mammal 14

viruses germs that do harm in the body by invading and destroying cells and turning them into virus-making factories 86–87, 88, 89

vitamin essential nutrient required by body in small quantities. Does not provide energy or serve as a building block in the cell, but essential for the healthy functioning of the body. Most vitamins cannot be made in the body, but are found in sufficient quantities in a balanced diet 24, 52

voice box (also called larynx) short passageway in the throat that leads to the trachea (wind pipe). Sounds and speech originate from vibration of folded membranes, but other parts such as the mouth and nose cavity act as resonating chambers that give each human voice its characteristic sound 96

volcano mountain or hill that has opening(s) to the Earth's crust through which lava, steam and gases are expelled 10

W

wax (in the ear) ear wax is produced by special glands near the outside opening of the ear. Helps prevent dust and other foreign objects from entering the ear 74

white blood cells defender cells in the blood. The three main types are neutrophils, lymphocytes and macrophages 46, 60, 78–89

womb pear-shaped muscular bag inside a woman's body where a baby grows from a tiny ball of cells (also called the uterus) 96, 97, 98, 100, 102, 104

X

X chromosome (*krome-oh-soame*) female humans have two of these chromosomes, males only one. Known as a sex chromosome 107

Y

Y chromosome (*krome-oh-soame*) only male humans have this chromosome. Known as a sex chromosome 107

yeast microscopic creature made of a single cell, simplest form of fungus 33

The authors wish to thank the following people who gave advice, reference, useful criticism, and encouragement:

From the Imperial Cancer Research Fund

Sir Walter Bodmer, Director General; Dr David Forman, Cancer Epidemiology; Dr Tim Hunt, Cell Cycle Control Laboratory; Dr Suhale Islam, Molecular Modelling Laboratory; Members of the Biological Therapies Laboratory; Dr Denise Sheer, Human Cytogenetics Laboratory; Rose Watson Dip EM, Cell Biology Laboratory

Dr Heather Couper, Pioneer Productions, Buckinghamshire; Dr Jonathan Freidman, St George's Hospital Medical School, London; David Sealy, Department of Palaeontology, Natural History Museum, London; Gregory Snell BDSc; Dr Gordon Stamp, Department of Histopathology, Royal Postgraduate Medical School, Hammersmith Hospital, London; Dr Caroline Wigley, Department of Anatomy, Guy's Hospital, London; Professor Lewis Wolpert, University College, London

National Aeronautics and Space Administration, Houston, Texas, USA